William Shakespeare

The Tragedy of
CORIOLANUS

New Kittredge Shakespeare

William Shakespeare

The Tragedy of
CORIOLANUS

Editor
Jeffrey Kahan
University of La Verne

Series Editor
James H. Lake
*Louisiana State University,
Shreveport*

The Tragedy of Coriolanus
© 2012 Focus Publishing
Edited by George Lyman Kittredge.
Used with permission from the heirs to the Kittredge estate.
New material by Jeffrey Kahan used with permission.

Focus Publishing/R. Pullins Company
PO Box 369
Newburyport MA 01950
www.pullins.com

Cover Design by Guy Wetherbee | Elk Amino Design, New England | elkaminodesign.com

Cover illustration: Venturia pleading with Coriolanus to call off his planned attack on Rome (color lithograph). English School (20th century) / Private collection / The Stapleton Collection / Bridgeman Art Library International.

ISBN: 978-1-58510-349-2

Library of Congress Cataloging-in-Publication Data

Shakespeare, William, 1564-1616.
   [Coriolanus]
   The tragedy of Coriolanus / William Shakespeare ; editor Jeffrey Kahan.
      p. cm.
   Includes bibliographical references.
   ISBN 978-1-58510-349-2
   1. Coriolanus, Cnaeus Marcius--Drama. 2. Generals--Drama. 3.
Rome--Drama. I. Kahan, Jeffrey, 1964- II. Title.
   PR2805.A2K34 2012
   822.3'3--dc23

                                    2012010302
Printed in the United States of America

10 9 8 7 6 5 4 3 2 1

0312V

TABLE OF CONTENTS

Publisher's Note

George Lyman Kittredge was one of the foremost American Shakespeare scholars of the 20th century. The New Kittredge Shakespeare, builds on his celebrated scholarship and extensive notes. Each edition contains a new, updated introduction, with comments on contemporary film versions of the play, new and revised notes, including performance notes, an essay on reading the play as performance, plus topics for discussion and an annotated bibliography and filmography. For this an accomplished Shakespeare and film scholar has been commissioned to modernize each volume.

The series focuses on understanding the language and allusions in the play as well as encountering Shakespeare as performance. The audience ranges from students at all levels, as well as to readers interested in encountering the text in the context of performance on stage or film.

Ron Pullins, Publisher
Newburyport, 2009

Introduction to the Kittredge Edition

CORIOLANUS was first printed in the Folio of 1623. The Folio text is in one sense good, for it goes back to an authentic copy; but there are abundant errata, and in many passages of verse the division into lines is incorrect. Mere misprints almost correct themselves... [Setting verse presents a greater challenge.] In the late period to which the play obviously belongs, Shakespeare handled his verse with great freedom. When, therefore, a line seems hypermetrical, one cannot be sure that the printer has gone astray. Mislineation is, in general, easy to adjust, even when verse is printed as prose or prose as verse. Now and then, however, the question arises whether Shakespeare intended a passage to be verse or prose. There is, for example, a bad muddle in the Folio text of 2.1.144-47:

> Within Corioles Gates: where he hath wonne,
> With Fame, a Name to *Martius Caius:*
> These in honor followes *Martius Caius Coriolanus.*
> Welcome to Rome, renowned *Coriolanus.*

A curious instance of confusing omission occurs in 2.3.227-28, where the Folio reads:

> And Nobly nam'd, so twice being Censor,
> Was his great Ancestor.

Here North's Plutarch has led editors gradually to what must be in effect the right reading. The passage which Shakespeare was versifying runs as follows: 'Of the same house were *Publius & Quintus,* who brought to ROME their best water they had by conduites. *Censorinus* also came of that familie, that was so surnamed, because the people had chosen him *Censor* twise.'

As evidence for the date of composition, two supposed allusions to the play have been cited—one from Ben Jonson and one from Robert Armin.

Cominius the Consul, celebrating the exploits of Coriolanus (2.2.69) says that at the age of sixteen he won the oaken garland in the battle against Tarquin, and that

> In the brunt of seventeen battles since
> He lurch'd all swords of the garland.   (2.2.96-97)

That is, 'he robbed all other warriors of the prize for valour.' Ben Jonson uses the same phrase figuratively in *Epicœne; or, The Silent Women*: 'You have lurch'd your friends of the better half of the garland' (V.4). *Epicœne* was first acted in 1609. If Jonson was echoing Shakespeare, this fixes one limit for the date of CORIOLANUS. But 'garland' in a figurative sense is not uncommon and 'lurch' for 'cheat' or 'rob' was a familiar colloquialism. The other supposed quotation, rather more striking, occurs in Robert Armin's preface to his poem *The Italian Taylor and his Boy*, printed in 1609: 'A strange time of taxation, wherein euery Pen and inck-horne Boy will throw vp his Cap at the hornes of the Moone in censure, although his wit hang there, not returning vnless monthly in the wane.' Compare 1.1.196-97:

> They threw their caps
> As they would hang them on the horns o' th' moon.

Armin certainly acted in some of Shakespeare's plays, for his name stands in the list of 'the Principall Actors' in the First Folio. He joined the company about 1599 and still belonged to it in 1610, when he was one of 'the principall Comœdians' in Jonson's *Alchemist*. His special talent was for Clowns and Fools. There is good reason to believe that he played Dogberry in *Much Ado*. What part he took (if any) in CORIOLANUS is a matter of conjecture. Menenius has been suggested, but that is no clown's rôle. One of the comic Volscian servingmen seems more likely—perhaps the Third (4.5.13). At all events, Armin's head was crammed with scraps of plays, as his pamphlets show, and such a wild hyperbole as this of caps on the moon's horns would doubtless take his fancy. Thus he is a better witness than usual. Yet all such evidence, however entertaining, is indecisive. Style and metre are far better tests, and these put CORIOLANUS beyond question in Shakespeare's latest period. Sometime in 1608, perhaps soon after *Antony and Cleopatra*, satisfies all the conditions.

For material Shakespeare went to the life of Coriolanus in Sir Thomas North's translation of Plutarch (1595). He uses North in the Roman plays as he uses Holinshed in the English 'histories' and tragedies: in some passages he merely turns North's eloquent prose into verse; in others he takes a suggestion and elaborates it. As to characters, Plutarch describes and Shakespeare creates.

His use of North may be illustrated by Menenius' fable (1.1.79) of the Belly and the Members. In North this runs as follows:

> On a time all the members of mans body did rebell against the
> bellie, complaining of it, that it onely remained in the middest of
> the bodie, without doing any thing, neither did beare any labour to
> the maintenaunce of the rest: whereas all other partes and members
> did labour paynefully, & were very carefull to satisfie the appetites
> and desires of the bodie. And so the bellie, all this notwithstanding
> laughed at their follie, and sayed. It is true, I first receiue all meates
> that norish mans bodie: but afterwardes I send it againe to the
> norishment of other partes of the same. Euen so (quoth he) o you,
> my maisters, and citizens of ROME: the reason is alike betweene the

Senate & you. For matters being wel digested, & their counsells throughly examined, touching the benefite of the common wealth: the Senatours are cause of the common commoditie that commeth vnto euery one of you.

The fable is of Oriental origin. It made its way somehow into Roman history of the legendary period and is attached to Menenius by Livy (ii, 32) and Plutarch. Camden tells it in his *Remaines* (1605). Of course Shakespeare could read Livy.

Editor's Note

Kittridge's Introduction dwells on both the historical sources and the theatrical context of the play—note, for example, his references to Plutarch, Livy, Ben Jonson's *Epicœne* and *The Alchemist*. This information may be daunting to some students but is ultimately useful, in that it reminds students that Shakespeare's imaginative powers were harnessed to scholarly practices and to the commercial realities of a highly competitive theatrical marketplace. I have taken the liberty of pruning Kittredge's examples of the play's misprints and word stresses. My rationale for the lacunae is as follows: While the material is useful to other textual editors and Shakespearean scholars, the information can be off-putting to students and does not necessarily enhance their appreciation of the play itself. Kittredge supplied no notes to his original edition of the play. The information I have supplied is designed to explain the text in a straightforward way and to offer examples of the play in performance.

— Jeffrey Kahan, 2012

INTRODUCTION TO THE FOCUS EDITION

CORIOLANUS is one of Shakespeare's Roman plays, based upon the writings of the historian Plutarch. However, it is not necessary for students to be familiar with Roman history to understand the events of the play; in the main, *Coriolanus* is not a dusty history but a timeless tragedy; vested with Roman triumphs, feted by Roman's citizens, Coriolanus is a soldier who comes to see himself as a hero and then, after yet more triumphs and public acclamations, believes himself to be a kind of god. His subsequent fall from Olympian grace is abrupt; his ordeal to assert his humanity proves cheerless and fatal.

The godlike being known as "Coriolanus" can be said to be fashioned by the Romans. Born with the name Caius Martius, raised by a woman who finds only blood and battle praiseworthy, our protagonist thinks of himself as a killing machine. So too do the people of Rome. After he conquers the city of Corioli, Rome rewards him with a military triumph—a Roman version of a ticker-tape parade. As part of that public ceremony, the rulers of Rome strip away his old name and bestow a new identity, reflective of his latest military glory: Coriolanus. Martius accepts his new name with little complaint; but his defining moment comes not in victory but in defeat, and not among foreign foes, but among his own people. In order to become consul—the equivalent of kingly ruler of Rome—the victor of Corioli must wear a gown of humility and let the poor of Rome inspect his war wounds. It is part of an ancient custom of Rome, but the newly-minted Coriolanus objects. Why should he let these people poke and prod him as if he were a prize horse? He did not join the army with a view to being consul, but, given his patriotic service, why should he beg for what is rightfully his? Should Rome's greatest champion take the low road to gain high reward; should not principle outweigh ambition?

> MARTIUS   To brag unto them, "Thus I did, and thus!"
> Show them th' unaching scars which I should hide,
> As if I had receiv'd them for the hire
> Of their breath only! (2.2.143-46)

Martius' refusal to act properly and agreeably before people he considers inferior or inconsequential is vital to an understanding of his character. To play the humble supplicant is to deny his true nature, to favor expedience over principle. Only by maintaining his incorruptibility can he deny his mutability. Put simply, to be like the statued heroes and gods of Rome, he must be hard, cold and immoveable, an elemental force that demands worship. As the Volscians say of him: "He's the rock, the oak not to be wind-shaken" (5.2.103).

No wonder Martius feels that the regular rituals of Rome should be cast aside for him; he is not like other men, and certainly not one to curry their favor. He is unpleasant and uncomfortable in the presence of common Romans, and we can easily imagine him as more than half-relieved when the people accuse him of being a traitor. In a real sense, he is. In the words of Katherine Stockholder, "because he is unable to subordinate the image of himself to a deeply felt commitment to his country, [Martius] reveals his potentiality for treachery."[1] Indeed, when he fails to gain the consulship, he immediately terrorizes those he had hoped to govern: "There's some among you have beheld me fighting./Come try upon yourselves what you have seen me" (3.1.222-23). War against the Volscians is one thing, civil war against the common men and women of Rome is something entirely different, and even Martius' closest friends balk at his bloodthirsty proposal. By common consent, Rome's greatest hero is banished. Dishonored by those he least respects, Martius turns his back on the people of Rome: "There is," he says, "a world elsewhere" (3.3.135).

Or is there? Martius is now free to reinvent himself not by the confines of Roman custom but by the boundless stretches of the human imagination. Yet, Martius quickly discovers that leaving Rome is not the same as abjuring Roman identity. Coriolanus has been raised in Rome; his friends, family, wife, and child are left within its city walls. All he has known has been shaped by Roman tradition and its emphasis on confrontation. He is a warrior and, for a man so battle-scarred, his pride remains an open wound. If he cannot make war in the name of Rome, he will make war *on* Rome.

Volumnia: The Murderous Mother

We often refer to cities, boats, even cars, as female. But Rome herself is brutal, warlike, and expansionist, traits Shakespeare's England, and ancient Rome herself, would have associated more with the masculine than with the feminine. Why Coriolanus will not yield to the people of Rome is intimately connected to his masculinity. As Cominus states, at age sixteen, when Martius was a virgin in the ways of war, he distinguished himself by out-daring other men in violent exploits:

> In that day's feats,
>   When he might act the woman in the scene,
> He prov'd best man i' th' field...   (2.2.91-93)

In Martius' mind, meekness is a feminine quality, a quality that, in the violence of battle, may just get you killed: "There is no more mercy in him [Martius] than there is milk in a male tiger"(5.4.23-24). Further, meekness and femininity are hardly common traits to be found in Martius' household. From almost infancy, his mother Volumnia has instilled in her son a contempt for life and a love of violence. While this is to some degree understandable—like all great powers, Rome has her enemies—it is all too obvious that Martius is the victim of his mother's ambitions. In 1.3, we see Volumnia and her daughter-in-law, Virgilia, awaiting word of Martius' return from

---

1   Katherine Stockholder, "The Other Coriolanus." *PMLA*, 85.2 (March, 1970): 228-236; 232.

war. Virgilia understands what is expected of a traditional Roman maid. While her husband fights in the field, she is to sequester herself and to pass the time weaving and sewing. Volumnia, on the other hand, has never practiced traditional feminine virtues. She suggests that Virgilia visit neighbors or "sing, or express [herself] in a more comfortable sort" (1.3.1-2).

Indeed, it is clear that Volumnia has always wanted to be a soldier and now lives vicariously through her son's exploits. While her son and the army engage Aufidius and his warlike Volscians many miles from the city, Volumnia imagines herself in the thick of the battle, clashing swords and helms with the other combatants:

> Methinks I hear hither your husband's drum;
> See him pluck Aufidius down by th' hair;
> As children from a bear, the Volsces shunning him.
> Methinks I see him stamp thus, and call thus:
> 'Come on, you cowards! You were got in fear,
> Though you were born in Rome.' His bloody brow
> With his mail'd hand then wiping, forth he goes,
> Like to a harvestman that's task'd to mow
> Or all or lose his hire.   (1.3.26-34)

Volumnia may be a Roman matron, but she is best suited to be a warrior, perhaps one of the legendary Amazonians, female warriors who cut their right breast off so as to string a bow or throw a spear without physical limitation or obstruction. For Volumnia to become the great champion of Rome she has always dreamed of being, her son must be her willing servitor and sacrificial victim, a child consumed in the belly of her growing ambition. Certainly, Coriolanus' ultimate decision to die for Rome is umbilically tied both to his mother and to the stern loyalty demanded of Rome, described as an "unnatural dam" (3.1.291).

Political Considerations

William Hazlitt, the early nineteenth-century essayist, understood that Coriolanus' greatness depends upon an acceptance of cruelty, injustice, and inhumanity as the natural order of things:

> "The whole dramatic moral of Coriolanus is, that those who have
> little shall have less, and that those who have much shall take all
> that others have left. The people are poor, therefore they ought to
> be starved. They are slaves, therefore they ought to be beaten. They
> work hard, therefore they ought to be treated like beasts of burden.
> They are ignorant; therefore they ought not to be allowed to feel
> that they want food, or clothing, or rest, that they are enslaved,
> oppressed, and miserable."[2]

---

2   William Hazlitt, *Examiner*, December 15, 1816, as cited in *Hazlitt on Theatre*, ed. William Archer. (New York: Hill and Wang, 1957), 112-117; 116.

It may seem that Hazlitt is setting aside the play to talk about politics, but he may be on to something here. As the ancient Greek historian Polybius (ca. 203–120 BC) makes clear, the political health of a country is integrally related to the virtues and defects of its heroes and leaders:

> "The test of true virtue in a man surely resides in his capacity to bear with spirit and with dignity the most complete transformations of fortune, and the same principle should apply to our judgement of states. And so, since I could find no greater or more violent changes of fortune in our time than those which befell the Romans, I have reserved this place in my history for my study of their constitution."[3]

In this light, Menenius' tale of the belly (1.1.79-136), in which he argues that the health of a society can only be maintained when the limbs (i.e. the workers) do as they are told and wait patiently for their reward, is not merely to discuss the whys and wherefores of grain distribution. It is to set the hungry plebeians apart from the monastic discipline of Martius, to compare their fearful wavering to his noble persistence, their sickly condition to his godlike grandeur. It is, above all, to diagnose the true illness of Rome herself: the nobility's ignoble capitulation to "the rule of the mob."[4] As Martius presages, in feeding the famished of Rome the nobility "nourish 'gainst our Senate/ The cockle of rebellion, insolence, sedition" (3.1.69-70).

Given the distaste Martius and other aristocrats have for the common folk of Rome, it would seem that democracy is not Rome's—nor, by extension, Shakespeare's—preferred mode of government. The possibility that the Western world's greatest dramatist is firmly against the quintessentially Western ideal of democracy is, to say the least, disquieting. Yet from the first, Shakespeare designed the play as a tragedy, a genre which requires that his audience sympathize with the protagonist. If Shakespeare had some sympathy for Martius, as the generics of tragedy necessitate, then we must admit the possibility that Shakespeare approved of Martius' greatness and expected his audience to be saddened by his death.

Oh, how times have changed! As Robert Hanks wrote recently in a review of an RSC production of the play, "sure, he [Martius] wins battles, but would you want this psycho in charge [of the state]?"[5] At the very least we can say that many of us do not identify with Martius, that our own sympathies are not in accord with those of Shakespeare's audience, nor, perhaps, in accord with Shakespeare himself. Without the ability to question Shakespeare, we're likely never to know his personal opinion on this matter. He might have sympathized with his heroic creation; on the other hand, Coriolanus might be a prime example of what Coleridge called Shakespeare's "wonderfully philosophic impartiality."[6]

3   Polybius, *The Rise of the Roman Empire*, Introduction, F. W. Walbank; trans. Ian Scott-Kilvert. (Oxford: Oxford University Press, 1979), 302.

4   Ibid., 350.

5   Robert Hanks, *The Independent*, March 8, 2007.

6   Samuel Taylor Coleridge, *Coleridge's Writings on Shakespeare*, ed. Terence Hawkes (New York: Capricorn Books/G.P. Putnam's Sons, 1959), 251.

Stage and Film History

Since Shakespeare's day, *Coriolanus* has been adapted to mirror our ever-evolving interests and concerns. In the Restoration, the play was revised by Nahum Tate to reflect, as he put it in the title, *The Ingratitude of a Common-Wealth; Or, The Fall of Caius Martius Coriolanus*. In Tate's view, Coriolanus was right to reject the Roman mob because dependence "on the uncertain Crowd" led to anarchy. He therefore suggested that the moral of the play was "to Recommend Submission and Adherence to Establisht Lawful Power."[7] The more democratically-minded British poet James Thomson staged his own version of the play in 1745. In his version, Volumnia, therein renamed Venturia, accuses her son of destroying democratic Rome with tyrannical ambition. When Coriolanus refuses to leave the Volscian camp, she promises to kill herself before she will see her son ruling as Rome's tyrant. In Thomas Sheridan's version, performed in Dublin in 1752, Coriolanus' contempt for the citizens was redirected to just the tribunes; the underlying message was that our hero loved the people but hated their cowardly and conniving representatives.[8]

The greatest Coriolanus of the eighteenth century was John Philip Kemble. John Howard Payne vividly recalled that Kemble's "person derived majesty from a scarlet robe which he managed with inimitable dignity. The Roman energy of his deportment, the seraphic grace of his gesture, and the movements of his perfect self-possession displayed the great mind, daring to command, and disdaining to solicit, admiration."[9] A less-appreciative William Hazlitt noted that Kemble's Martius conveyed his displeasure by raising his nose in the air, like a man "who is about to sneeze."[10]

Americans have had their say as well. The nineteenth-century American actor Edwin Forrest portrayed Coriolanus not as a would-be demagogue but as a champion of democracy:

> "What unconsciously delighted Forrest in *Coriolanus*, and what he represented with consummate felicity and force of nature, was that his aristocracy was of the true democratic type; that is, it rested on a consciousness of intrinsic personal worth and superiority, not on conventional privilege and prescription. He loathed and launched his scorching invectives against the commonalty not because they were plebeians and he was a patrician, but because of the revolting

7   Nahum Tate, *The Ingratitude of a Common-Wealth; Or, The Fall of Caius Martius Coriolanus* (London: T.M. for Joseph Hindmarsh, 1682), 2; rpt. In Brian Vickers (ed.), *William Shakespeare: The Critical Heritage* (1974; rpt. London: Francis and Taylor, 2005), I: 330-331.

8   See Esther K. Sheldon, Sheridan's *Coriolanus*: An 18th-Century Compromise." *Shakespeare Quarterly* 14.2 (Spring, 1963), pp. 153-161, in which she notes that Thomson's version was not an adaptation, but an entirely new play. Sheridan muddled Acts 1-2 of Shakespeare with Acts 3-5 of Thomson.

9   *Actors and Actresses of Great Britain: The Kembles*, Eds. Brander Mathews and Laurence Hutton (Boston: L.C. Page & Company, 1900), 85-86.

10   William Hazlitt, *Examiner*, December 15, 1816, as cited in *Hazlitt on Theatre*, 117.

opposition of their baseness to his loftiness, of their sycophancy to his pride, of their treacherous fickleness to his adamantine steadfastness."[11]

In short, Coriolanus was great because he was the embodiment of the American Dream, a self-made man who disliked anyone who told him what to do. When Forrest's Martius told the Roman mob that there is a "world elsewhere"(3.3.144), his audience, many of whom were new to the country, understood him well enough. America was Martius' "world elsewhere," a place where a man might be himself and reach his true potential.

In the nineteenth—and for much of the twentieth—century, the play lost its way. Edmund Kean, an actor who generally played to the middle and lower classes, tried and failed as the aristocratic Martius; Charles Macready met with greater success, but his production relied more upon stage spectacle than interpretative performance. Upon Martius' return from Corioli, for example, the stage was filled with over 300 extras, dressed as Roman citizen from all classes.[12] The effect on one playgoer was such that she lamented that she was too close to the stage to take in fully the wonderful visuals of the production:

> The effect given by the number of the mob, by the variety of action which seemed to give Shakespearian individuality to every member of it, is indescribable. The cowed, degraded appearance of the Volscians in the Triumph was very striking; *Coriolanus* sitting at the hearth of Aufidius [is] as fine a picture as can be imagined. Still I was too near the stage to judge of the full effect, or even to see the whole of the fine scenes.[13]

In 1901, Sir Henry Irving mounted the play at the Lyceum to hostile reviews: *The Athenaeum* (April 20, 1901) wrote: "'Coriolanus' is not dramatically stirring, and since the days of Kemble, it has been no great favourite with managers"; *The Saturday Review* (April 27, 1901) thought that Martius, as interpreted by Irving, was "a character wasted," and that Ellen Terry's Volumnia was "not less disastrously wasted than Sir Henry." In 1951, CBS TV brought the play to the small screen, but without much success. Jack Gould of the *New York Times* called it "not very exciting"; Richard Greene's Martius was "virtually expressionless."[14]

The acclaimed eastern European playwright Bertolt Brecht began revising the play in 1956. In his unfinished version, the play opens with Martius planning to quell a revolt of the starving plebeians; the plan is interrupted by a Volscian attack.

---

11   William Rounseville Alger. *Life of Edwin Forrest, the American Tragedian: The American Tragedian.* 2 vols. (Philadelphia: J.B. Lippincott & Co., 1877), 2: 762.

12   *Sunday Times*, March 18, 1838.

13   Frances Williams-Wynn, *Diaries of a Lady of Quality from 1797 to 1844*. Ed. Abraham Hayward. 2nd Ed. (London: Longman, Green, Longman, Roberts, & Green, 1864), 304.

14   *Shakespeare on Television: An Anthology of Essays and Reviews*. Eds. J.C. Bulman and H.R. Coursen (Hanover and London: University Press of New England, 1988), 237-238.

He is elected as consul but the people withdraw their endorsement when they learn of Martius' plans against them. The citizens do not cower when word comes that Coriolanus has joined the Volsces. Rather, they arm and prepare to meet him in battle, but Volumnia "moves her son to turn back." She then returns to a thankless Rome.[15] A 1961 production at Stratford Ontario (dir. Michael Langham) set *Coriolanus* in the French Revolution, but, despite the brilliance of Paul Scofield's Martius, the production was met with some hostility. Jean Beraud of Montreal's *La Presse* thought that "the idea of transferring the action from Rome to a sort of Napoleonic stage is disturbing. Frequent anachronisms mix the ridiculous with the sublime."[16]

The BBC's 1984 TV version has received mixed reviews. John Engstrom of the *Boston Globe* lamented that much of the politics was cut but thought that Alan Howard's Martius was "peerless"; on the other hand, Katherine Duncan-Jones, writing in the *Times Literary Supplement*, thought that Howard was "seriously miscast as Coriolanus" and that the production as a whole "fails ever to rise to real excitement." Maurice Charney, writing in *Shakespeare on Film Newsletter*, suggested, with faint disapproval, that were the BBC to do the play again, it would now "have a better sense of what the public wants."[17]

A 1988 New York City Public Theatre production, directed by Stephen Berkoff and starring Christopher Walken as Martius, attempted to bring *Coriolanus* into a contemporary setting: "Christopher Walken's [Martius] was a modern urbanite. Well-dressed in 1980s high fashion, he wore a long, black leather overcoat, black silk shirt, and black trousers," as if he had stepped out "from the pages of *GQ*."[18] Berkoff returned to the play in 1991 and again in 1995 as its director and far-less debonair lead actor. Goose-steeping, bellowing, constantly enflamed and utterly unsympathetic, Berkoff makes for a convincing Neo-Nazi hooligan, never happier than when he is in battle. Still, he is so aggressively unlikeable that many viewers may hate him, and feel, as a consequence, great relief when he is finally killed. Further, it's difficult to believe that Berkoff, who is a physically slight actor, is capable of creating bodily menace.

A 1995 RSC production (dir. David Thacker) cast twenty-six year old Toby Stephens as Martius, described by Charles Spencer as a beguiling "fascist brute who makes impressionable women go weak at the knees."[19] Still other directors have related Coriolanus' übermasculinity to a homoerotic impulse. A 1996 production at the Oregon Shakespeare Festival (dir. Tony Taccone) featured a "detailed macho world: pistols, automatic rifles, grenades, swords, knives, camouflage, hand-to-hand

15   See Brecht's "Plan of the Play," in *Bertolt Brecht: Collected Plays*. Eds. Ralph Manheim and John Willett. 9 Vols. (New York: Pantheon/Random House, 1972),9:375-376.

16   As cited in the *Saskatoon Star-Phoenix*, June 21, 1961.

17   *Shakespeare on Television: An Anthology of Essays and Reviews*, 304-306.

18   William Over, "The Public Theatre *Coriolanus.*" *Shakespeare Quarterly* 41 (1990): 365-368; 366.

19   Charles Spencer, *Daily Telegraph*, August 12, 1995.

combat, bulging groin pouches, black leather, blood, blasts of heavy metal."[20] Of William Houston's Martius (RSC, 2007; dir. Greg Doran), Charles Spencer wrote, "There is also more than a hint of homosexual attraction in his dealings with his great Volscian adversary Tullus Aufidius… When they aren't fighting, they are constantly hugging, in a manly sort of way, of course."[21] In Berkoff's 1991 version, Aufidius was, in the words of the director, a "hard boy homosexual closeted mother-fucker."[22] In the Ralph Fiennes-directed *Coriolanus* (2011), our hero is by turns hateful and pitiable; a once-cuddly puppy raised by a she-wolf.

Compared to *Hamlet* and *Macbeth*, *Coriolanus* is staged infrequently, but, if you have a chance to see it, pay close attention to Martius' death, which, even in recent memory, has been variously interpreted. Alan Howard's Martius (RSC, 1977; dir. Terry Hands) taunted the Volscians to cut him to pieces—"Come on, all do it, all do it"—perhaps to deny Aufidius the honor of defeating him in single combat.[23] In the 1984 BBC TV version (dir Elijah Moshinsky), Martius (again played by Alan Howard) expressed a thrilling, perhaps even orgasmic, joy in death. In Steven Berkoff's 1991 version, Martius thrills to hear the catalogue of those he has killed. He is thereafter encircled and stabbed by the Volscian lords, Aufidius administering a *coup de grace*. But the beast will not die quickly: Martius pulls the weapon from his belly and, with his dying breath, points it at Aufidius. At the climax of a 2002 RSC production (Dir. David Farr), Martius (Greg Hicks) is "felled by a cheating bullet from behind. Twice he drags himself to his feet to continue the contest and twice more he's shot."[24] Perhaps the most interesting recent interpretation was staged at the Olde Globe, San Diego, 2009 (dir. Darko Tresnjak), in which Martius acquiesces to his mother's demand for surrender by placing his pistol in her hands.[25] Moments later he is killed by Aufidius and his men. On Volumnia's return to Rome, she is feted as the new Martius:

> the life of Rome!
> Call all your tribes together, praise the gods,
> And make triumphant fires; strew flowers before them.
> Unshout the noise that banish'd Martius;
> Repeal him with the welcome of his mother.   (5.5.1-5)

Volumnia has given birth to her ambition; she is at last the hero and savior of Rome. Yet, she stands friendless amidst the fanfare, silently confronting the too-cold reality that she has doomed her son to death in order to elevate her own social standing.

— Jeffrey Kahan, University of La Verne

20   Joe Adcock, *Seattle Post Intelligencer*, July 9, 1996.

21   Charles Spencer, *The Daily Telegraph*, March 8, 2007.

22   Steven Berkoff, *Coriolanus in Deutschland* (London: Amber Lane Press, 1992), 111.

23   David Daniell, *'Coriolanus' in Europe* (London: Athlone Press, 1980), 40-41, 166.

24   Paul Taylor, *The Independent*, December 4, 2002.

25   On the night I saw it, Martius was played by Steven Marzolf, who was substituting for Greg Derelian, but in all likelihood the stage business remained the same.

THE TRAGEDY OF CORIOLANUS

DRAMATIS PERSONAE

Caius Martius, afterwards *Caius Martius Coriolanus.*
Titus Lartius ⎱
Cominius ⎰ Generals against the Volscians.
Menenius Agrippa, friend to *Coriolanus.*
Sicinius Velutus ⎱
Junius Brutus ⎰ Tribunes of the People.
Young Martius, son to *Coriolanus.*
A Roman Herald.
Nicanor, a Roman.
Tullus Aufidius, General of the Volscians.
Lieutenant to *Aufidius.*
Conspirators with *Aufidius.*
Adrian, a Volscian.
A Citizen of Antium.
Two Volscian Guards.

Volumnia, mother to *Coriolanus.*
Virgilia, wife to *Coriolanus.*
Valeria, friend to *Virgilia.*
Gentlewoman, attending on *Virgilia.*

Senators (Roman and Volscian), Patricians, Ædiles, Lictors, Soldiers, Citizens, Messengers, Servants to Aufidius, Attendants.

SCENE.—Rome and the neighbourhood; Corioles (Corioli) and the neighbourhood; Antium.

Steven Berkoff's Coriolanus, recorded at the Globe Theatre in Tokyo in 1997, began with citizens wielding baseball bats and screaming and shouting.

ACT I

SCENE I. [*Rome. A street.*]†

Enter a company of mutinous Citizens, with staves, clubs, and other weapons.

I CITIZEN	Before we proceed any further, hear me speak.
ALL	Speak, speak!
I CITIZEN	You are all resolv'd rather to die than to famish?
ALL	Resolv'd, resolv'd!
I CITIZEN	First, you know Caius Martius is chief enemy to the people. 5
ALL	We know't, we know't!
I CITIZEN	Let us kill him, and we'll have corn at our own price. Is't a verdict?

ACT I. SCENE I.
3. **rather to die than to famish**: From the shortage of food, which Rome has in ready supply. See line 7, below. 5. **chief enemy**: It is unclear that Martius controls the supply of grain, and further, some citizens do not believe that he is entirely bad. See line 20 and 22. Nonetheless, he is clearly against feeding the poor. See 174-86. 7-8. **Is't a verdict**: Do you agree?

† The play can be staged in a traditional Roman setting, but it doesn't have to be. Berkoff's 1988 New York Public Theater production began with citizens wielding baseball bats and screaming and shouting "whenever their collective will is thwarted" (Gary Willis, *The New York Review of Books*, January 19, 1989); director Richard Rose (Stratford, Ontario, 1997) had his mob dressed in "hard hats, welder's masks," and, armed with "crude weapons," looked like they had just come from Gdansk Shipyard, birthplace of Poland's Solidarity Movement (Terry Doran, *Buffalo News*, July 2, 1997).

ALL	No more talking on't! Let it be done! Away, away!
2 CITIZEN	One word, good citizens. 10
1 CITIZEN	We are accounted poor citizens, the patricians good. What authority surfeits on would relieve us. If they would yield us but the superfluity while it were wholesome, we might guess they relieved us humanely; but they think we are too dear. The leanness that afflicts us, the object of our misery, is as an inventory to particularize their abundance; our sufferance is a gain to them. Let us revenge this with our pikes ere we become rakes; for the gods know I speak this in hunger for bread, not in thirst for revenge.
2 CITIZEN	Would you proceed especially against Caius Martius? 20
1 CITIZEN	Against him first. He's a very dog to the commonalty.
2 CITIZEN	Consider you what services he has done for his country?
1 CITIZEN	Very well, and could be content to give him good report for't but that he pays himself with being proud.
2 CITIZEN	Nay, but speak not maliciously. 25
1 CITIZEN	I say unto you, what he hath done famously, he did it to that end. Though soft-conscienc'd men can be content to say it was for his country, he did it to please his mother and to be partly proud, which he is, even to the altitude of his virtue.
2 CITIZEN	What he cannot help in his nature, you account a vice in 30 him. You must in no way say he is covetous.
1 CITIZEN	If I must not, I need not be barren of accusations. He hath faults (with surplus) to tire in repetition. *Shouts within.*
	What shouts are these? The other side o' th' city is risen. Why stay we prating here? To th' Capitol! 35
ALL	Come, come!
1 CITIZEN	Soft! who comes here?
	Enter Menenius Agrippa.

11-13. **poor citizens, the patricians good**: Citizens poor, thus bad; patricians rich, thus good.—**surfeits on would relieve us**: The excess would satisfy us. —**superfluity**: extra.—**wholesome**: fresh, unspoiled. 14. **too dear**: ironic. Too expensive to be wasted. 15-16. **an inventory to particularize their abundance**: a means by which to measure their wealth.—**sufferance**: pain, suffering. 17-18 **pikes... rakes**: pikes, poles with sharp heads, compared to farm rakes—thin, like the starved people. 21. **dog to the commonalty**: guard dog, which attacks the common people. 25. **maliciously**: falsely. 27. **soft-conscienc'd**: soft-hearted, weak brained. 29. **altitude**: high minded, lofty, ambitious. 31. **covetous**: greedy. 32. **be not barren of accusations**: We have yet other reasons for hating him. 33. **surplus**: recalling the extra food supply; see line 13. 35. **prating**: talking, wasting time, doing nothing. 37. **Soft**: Hold on.

2 CITIZEN	Worthy Menenius Agrippa, one that hath always lov'd the people.
1 CITIZEN	He's one honest enough. Would all the rest were so! 40
MENENIUS	What work's, my countrymen, in hand? Where go you With bats and clubs? The matter? Speak, I pray you.
2 CITIZEN	Our business is not unknown to th' Senate. They have had inkling this fortnight what we intend to do, which now we'll show 'em in deeds. They say poor suitors have strong breaths; they shall know we have strong arms too.
MENENIUS	Why, masters, my good friends, mine honest neighbours, Will you undo yourselves?
2 CITIZEN	We cannot, sir; we are undone already.
MENENIUS	I tell you, friends, most charitable care 50 Have the patricians of you. For your wants, Your suffering in this dearth, you may as well Strike at the heaven with your staves as lift them Against the Roman state; whose course will on The way it takes, cracking ten thousand curbs 55 Of more strong link asunder than can ever Appear in your impediment. For the dearth, The gods, not the patricians, make it, and Your knees to them (not arms) must help. Alack! You are transported by calamity 60 Thither where more attends you; and you slander The helms o' th' state, who care for you like fathers, When you curse them as enemies.
2 CITIZEN	Care for us? True indeed! They ne'er car'd for us yet: suffer us to famish, and their storehouses cramm'd with grain; 65 make edicts for usury, to support usurers; repeal daily any wholesome act established against the rich, and provide more piercing statutes daily to chain up and restrain the

38-40. **lov'd the people**: Might be meant ironically. See Menenius's tale of the belly speech (lines 79-97) and insults throughout 2.1, below. 41. **What work's**: What are you doing? 44. **inkling**: hints. 48. **undo**: ruin, destroy. 50. **charitable**: careful, kind. 52. **dearth**: famine, contradicted by the abundance of the food supply. 53-54. **Strike at the heaven…Roman state**: Twofold meaning: (1)You should blame the heavens rather than the state; (2) striking the state is about as effective as striking the heavens. In other words, it is a waste of time and strength to resist the power of Rome's godlike authority. 55. **curbs**: attempts to curb, change the direction, mindset, of the state. 57. **impediment**: Your attempts to stop the authority and order of the state; possible pun of implements (weapons) with impediments (weakness). 58. **The gods**: blamed for the famine, as in the Hebrew God's curse on the Egyptians or Apollo's wasting of the Greeks at Troy with plague. 60. **transported by calamity**: carried away by emotions during a time of crisis. 61. **more attends you**: More disasters await you, but these will be of your own doing. Rome will put down your insurrection. 65-69. **cramm'd with grain…usurers;… restrain the poor**: A set of grievances in which the citizens argue that the state seems to only care for the rich.

poor. If the wars eat us not up, they will; and there's all
the love they bear us.   70

MENENIUS   Either you must
Confess yourselves wondrous malicious
Or be accus'd of folly. I shall tell you
A pretty tale. It may be you have heard it;
But since it serves my purpose, I will venture   75
To stale't a little more.

2 CITIZEN   Well, I'll hear it, sir; yet you must not think to fob off our
disgrace with a tale. But an't please you, deliver.

MENENIUS   There was a time when all the body's members
Rebell'd against the belly; thus accus'd it: 80
That only like a gulf it did remain
I' th' midst o' th' body, idle and unactive,
Still cupboarding the viand, never bearing
Like labor with the rest; where th' other instruments
Did see and hear, devise, instruct, walk, feel,   85
And, mutually participate, did minister
Unto the appetite and affection common
Of the whole body. The belly answer'd.

2 CITIZEN   Well, sir, what answer made the belly?

MENENIUS   Sir, I shall tell you. With a kind of smile,   90
Which ne'er came from the lungs, but even thus—
For look you, I may make the belly smile
As well as speak—it tauntingly replied
To th' discontented members, the mutinous parts
That envied his receipt; even so most fitly   95
As you malign our senators for that
They are not such as you.

2 CITIZEN   Your belly's answer? What?
The kingly crowned head, the vigilant eye,
The counsellor heart, the arm our soldier,
Our steed the leg, the tongue our trumpeter,   100
With other muniments and petty helps
In this our fabric, if that they—

72-73. **malicious...folly**: Menenius accuses them of being mean or stupid. 77. **fob off**: distract, trick us; though, that may well be his intention. See lines 139-43, below. 79. **There was a time**: Menenius talks to them like they are children. The story, in which the state is represented as a body, soon unravels. See commentary at 1.1.118, 1.1.139 below. 81. **gulf**: pit. 82. **unactive**: inactive. 90. **smile**: Menenius subtly allows the belly to become the face and voice of the body politic. 94. **members**: arms, legs, extremities of the body, or, in the case of Rome, her citizens, who do all the work. 95. **envied his receipt**: envied his act of receiving all the food, of being full. 101. **muniments**: furnishing, playing on covering the body, in line 102, below. 102. **fabric**: body, covered with clothing.

MENENIUS	What then?
	Fore me, this fellow speaks! What then? What then?
2 CITIZEN	Should by the cormorant belly be restrain'd,
	Who is the sink o' th' body—
MENENIUS	Well, what then? 105
2 CITIZEN	The former agents, if they did complain,
	What could the belly answer?
MENENIUS	I will tell you;
	If you'll bestow a small (of what you have little)
	Patience awhile, you'st hear the belly's answer.
2 CITIZEN	Y'are long about it.
MENENIUS	Note me this, good friend: 110
	Your most grave belly was deliberate,
	Not rash like his accusers, and thus answer'd:
	"True is it, my incorporate friends," quoth he,
	"That I receive the general food at first
	Which you do live upon; and fit it is, 115
	Because I am the storehouse and the shop
	Of the whole body. But, if you do remember,
	I send it through the rivers of your blood
	Even to the court, the heart, to th' seat o' th' brain,
	And, through the cranks and offices of man, 120
	The strongest nerves and small inferior veins
	From me receive that natural competency
	Whereby they live. And though that all at once
	You, my good friends"—This says the belly. Mark me.
2 CITIZEN	Ay, sir, well, well.
MENENIUS	"Though all at once cannot 125
	See what I do deliver out to each,
	Yet I can make my audit up, that all
	From me do back receive the flour of all
	And leave me but the bran." What say you to't?
2 CITIZEN	It was an answer. How apply you this? 130
MENENIUS	The senators of Rome are this good belly,

---

102. **What then**: Along with expressions at lines 89, 97 and 110, the citizens are clamorous, like children, anxious to hear how the story turns out. 106. **former agents**: The aforesaid arms and legs, etc. of the body. 112. **rash**: hasty. 118. **rivers of your blood**: A belly does not, as Menenius admits, store anything, but processes and distributes it immediately. That is not the case in Rome, where the people are starving and the city is crammed with food stores. 126. **deliver out to each**: distribute the food to each part of the body. 127. **audit up**: my account, my story. 129. **bran**: the inedible part of grain.

And you the mutinous members. For, examine
Their counsels and their cares, digest things rightly
Touching the weal o' th' common, you shall find
No public benefit which you receive   135
But it proceeds or comes from them to you,
And no way from yourselves. What do you think,
You, the great toe of this assembly?

2 CITIZEN   I the great toe? Why the great toe?

MENENIUS   For that, being one o' th' lowest, basest, poorest   140
Of this most wise rebellion, thou goest foremost.
Thou rascal, that art worst in blood to run,
Lead'st first to win some vantage.
But make you ready your stiff bats and clubs.
Rome and her rats are at the point of battle;   145
The one side must have bale.

                    Enter Caius Martius.[†]

                            Hail, noble Martius!

MARTIUS   Thanks. What's the matter, you dissentious rogues
That, rubbing the poor itch of your opinion,
Make yourselves scabs?

2 CITIZEN   We have ever your good word.

MARTIUS   He that will give good words to thee will flatter   150
Beneath abhorring. What would you have, you curs,
That like nor peace nor war? The one affrights you,
The other makes you proud. He that trusts to you,

---

132. **digest things rightly**: Suggests that the state is slow but thoughtful, deliberate and wise in its actions.
133. **And no way from yourselves**: Menenius' tone here shifts to an accusation. The government is the
source of all good; the people are ungrateful. 139-43. **great toe...vantage**: If a leg is an extremity far
away from the belly/center, then the toe is the most extreme of extremities, and, therefore, marginal,
useless. Again, contradicting the tale, in which all parts of the body benefited from the belly. Martius
is about to enter. It is possible that Menenius, who faced this hostile crowd alone, was merely wasting
time until Martius's arrival. Menenius not only calls Martius noble (line 146) but also calls the people
cowardly (line 186) and, like Martius, objects to giving the people any power. See line 204. 143.
vantage: advantage. 145. **Rome and her rats**: Rome versus the rats. Insult. The citizens are, in his
view, rats. 147. **dissentious**: quarrelsome. Insult. 148-50. **itch your opinion,/ Make yourselves scabs**:
Insult. They have fleas, and draw bloodly insurrection by their own actions. 151. **Beneath abhorring**:
Insult. Not worth the time of day. —**curs**: dogs.

[†]   What does Martius look like? For the 1954 New York Production at the Phoenix Theatre (dir.
John Houseman), "Robert Ryan plays him like an attractive, well-bred son of the upper classes
who despises the people more out of intellectual sluggishness than malice"(Brooks Atkinson, *New
York Times*, Jan. 24, 1954).

Where he should find you lions, finds you hares;
Where foxes, geese. You are no surer, no,   155
Than is the coal of fire upon the ice
Or hailstone in the sun. Your virtue is
To make him worthy whose offence subdues him,
And curse that justice did it. Who deserves greatness
Deserves your hate; and your affections are   160
A sick man's appetite, who desires most that
Which would increase his evil. He that depends
Upon your favors swims with fins of lead
And hews down oaks with rushes. Hang ye! Trust ye?
With every minute you do change a mind   165
And call him noble that was now your hate,
Him vile that was your garland. What's the matter
That in these several places of the city
You cry against the noble Senate, who
(Under the gods) keep you in awe, which else   170
Would feed on one another? What's their seeking?

MENENIUS   For corn at their own rates, whereof they say
                The city is well stor'd.

MARTIUS   Hang 'em! They say?
                They'll sit by th' fire and presume to know
                What's done i' th' Capitol, who's like to rise,   175
                Who thrives and who declines; side factions and give out
                Conjectural marriages, making parties strong
                And feebling such as stand not in their liking
                Below their cobbled shoes. They say there's grain enough?
                Would the nobility lay aside their ruth   180
                And let me use my sword, I'd make a quarry
                With thousands of these quarter'd slaves as high
                As I could pick my lance.

MENENIUS   Nay, these are almost thoroughly persuaded;
                For though abundantly they lack discretion,   185
                Yet are they passing cowardly. But I beseech you,
                What says the other troop?

154-57. **lions...hares;...hailstone in the sun**: cowardly and inconsistent. 158-62. **To make him worthy...increase his evil**: The people show poor judgment in their misplaced support. 170-71. **in awe, which else/ Would feed on one another**: The people, were it not for the authority of the state, would destroy themselves. Unnatural and mindless. 173. **well stor'd**: with food. See lines lines 11-14 above. 174-77. **They'll sit by th' fire and presume to know...Conjectural marriages**: gossips, who pretend that they know or have a say in the real dealings of the state. Martius implies they are marginal and unimportant, contradicted by lines 200-06, below. 178. **feebling**: enfeebled, weak. Insult. 179. **cobbled**: shoes made by a cobbler, working class. Insult. 180. **ruth**: pity. 186. **passing**: past all compare, exceedingly. 187. **troop**: The army, made up of the same poor citizens Coriolanus criticizes.

MARTIUS	They are dissolv'd. Hang 'em!
	They said they were anhungry; sigh'd forth proverbs—
	That hunger broke stone walls, that dogs must eat,
	That meat was made for mouths, that the gods sent not 190
	Corn for the rich men only. With these shreds
	They vented their complainings; which being answer'd
	And a petition granted them, a strange one,
	To break the heart of generosity
	And make bold power look pale, they threw their caps 195
	As they would hang them on the horns o' th' moon,
	Shouting their emulation.
MENENIUS	What is granted them?
MARTIUS	Five tribunes to defend their vulgar wisdoms
	Of their own choice. One's Junius Brutus,
	Sicinius Velutus, and I know not—'Sdeath! 200
	The rabble should have first unroof'd the city
	Ere so prevail'd with me. It will in time
	Win upon power and throw forth greater themes
	For insurrection's arguing.
MENENIUS	This is strange.
MARTIUS	Go get you home, you fragments! 205

Enter a Messenger hastily.

MESSENGER	Where's Caius Martius?
MARTIUS	Here. What's the matter?
MESSENGER	The news is, sir, the Volsces are in arms.
MARTIUS	I am glad on't. Then we shall ha' means to vent
	Our musty superfluity. See, our best elders.

Enter Cominius, Titus Lartius, with other Senators; Sicinius Velutus, Junius Brutus.

---

188. **anhungry**: hungry. 191. **Corn for the rich men only**: Reiterating the citizen's demand for more food; see 1.1.12, above. 192. **vented their complainings**: expressed. Possibly a pun, "farted their complaints." 195. **threw their caps**: tossed their hats in the air in celebration. 196. **horns o'th' moon**: unreachable and ever-changing. Echoing Menenius' warning at lines 53-54. 198. **Five tribunes**: The city of Rome has capitulated to the people's demands by allowing a temporary power share. We only see two tribunes in the play. 201. **unroof'd the city**: destroy Rome. 202. **It will in time**: Martius warns that sharing power with these worthless people will lead to great perils for all. 204. **This is strange**: Menenius objects to the logic of the power share and, thus, supports Martius' opinion. 206. **What's the matter**: When Martius asked this same question to the people (line 147), he did so scornfully. But here the question is addressed tactfully to a messenger from the aristocratic senate. 208-09. **vent/ Our musty superfluity**: flex our muscles in battle, shake off rust; also ironically echoing the people's complaint at line 13. Martius may be cryptic here. That battle will solve the problem by killing off the same citizens who now clamor for food.

Sicinius Velutus and Junius Brutus, shadowy conspirators, plot Coriolanus' downfall (*Coriolanus*, BBC 1984).

1 SENATOR	Martius, 'tis true that you have lately told us:	210
	The Volsces are in arms.	
MARTIUS	They have a leader,	
	Tullus Aufidius, that will put you to't.	
	I sin in envying his nobility;	
	And were I anything but what I am,	
	I would wish me only he.	
COMINIUS	You have fought together?	215
MARTIUS	Were half to half the world by th' ears, and he	
	Upon my party, I'd revolt, to make	
	Only my wars with him. He is a lion	
	That I am proud to hunt.	
1 SENATOR	Then, worthy Martius,	
	Attend upon Cominius to these wars.	220
COMINIUS	It is your former promise.	

212. **put you to't**: Put you to the test; test your mettle in battle. 215. **wish me only he**: A sign of respect, but also a faint hint of eroticism; note that he sees himself as only complete with Aufidius — "half to half" (line 216); anticipating Aufidius's speech at 4.5.95-120. See also 1.4.22, 1.6.29-30, 3.3.114, 4.3.27-28, 4.4.22, 4.5.210-11. 218-19. **lion/That I am proud to hunt**: Of course, the image insists that the lion is hunted. 220. **Attend upon Cominius to these wars**: That the great Martius is not the leader of the Romans in these wars is surprising, given everything we have heard about him. Cominius, we later learn, is Consul, a position of great honor and power in Rome. See 2.2.39. It is possible his deference to Cominius is added so that we see how easily he interacts with the aristocrats of the Senate. Coriolanus, to modernize the concept, has no problem with the officers of the army; it is the enlisted grunts, who come from the plebeian class, that he has issues with.

MARTIUS   Sir, it is,
          And I am constant. Titus Lartius, thou
          Shalt see me once more strike at Tullus' face.
          What, art thou stiff? Stand'st out?

LARTIUS   No, Caius Martius.
          I'll lean upon one crutch and fight with t'other   225
          Ere stay behind this business.

MENENIUS   O, true-bred!

1 SENATOR   Your company to th' Capitol, where I know
          Our greatest friends attend us.

LARTIUS   [*to Cominius*]   Lead you on.
          [*To Martius*] Follow Cominius. We must follow you;
          Right worthy you priority.

COMINIUS   Noble Martius!   230

1 SENATOR   [*to the Citizens*] Hence to your homes! be gone!

MARTIUS   Nay, let them follow.
          The Volsces have much corn. Take these rats thither
          To gnaw their garners. Worshipful mutiners,
          Your valor puts well forth. Pray follow.
                    Exeunt. Citizens steal away. Manent Sicinius and Brutus.

SICINIUS   Was ever man so proud as is this Martius?   235

BRUTUS   He has no equal.

SICINIUS   When we were chosen tribunes for the people—

BRUTUS   Mark'd you his lip and eyes?

SICINIUS   Nay, but his taunts!

BRUTUS   Being mov'd, he will not spare to gird the gods.

SICINIUS   Bemock the modest moon.   240

---

224. **art thou stiff**: with age, arthritis. 225. **I'll lean upon one crutch and fight with t'other**: A sign
of Roman bravery but also a sign of the role that military life plays in Rome. Shakespeare imagines
Coriolanus raised in a society that, properly speaking, is more Spartan than Roman. Roman citizenship
is linked to military service. See 1.3.5-22. 226. **true-bred**: Well bred, presumably, a warrior through
and through, a true Roman. 231. **Nay, let them follow**: Martius again insists that the people can satisfy
their hunger in battle, inferring that they can either die in battle or feed on the corpses of those they
kill. The fact that they "steal away" — i.e. sneak off — signals their cowardice or, depending upon your
conception of war, good sense. The common soldiers will also desert from the field when at Corioli. See
Martius' threat at 1.4.28-30. 238. **taunts**: The fact that the newly-elected tribunes are so thin-skinned
may have been added to suggest that they are more interested in gaining and maintain personal power
than in serving the people. 239. **gird**: sneer. 240. **Bemock the modest moon**: Find fault in even the
inoffensive moon. See 5.3.65, in which Martius talks to Valeria.

BRUTUS The present wars devour him! He is grown
Too proud to be so valiant.

SICINIUS   Such a nature,
Tickled with good success, disdains the shadow
Which he treads on at noon. But I do wonder
His insolence can brook to be commanded   245
Under Cominius.

BRUTUS   Fame, at the which he aims,
In whom already he's well grac'd, cannot
Better be held nor more attain'd than by
A place below the first; for what miscarries
Shall be the general's fault, though he perform   250
To th' utmost of a man, and giddy censure
Will then cry out of Martius, "O, if he
Had borne the business!"

SICINIUS   Besides, if things go well,
Opinion, that so sticks on Martius, shall
Of his demerits rob Cominius.

BRUTUS   Come.   255
Half all Cominius' honors are to Martius,
Though Martius earn'd them not; and all his faults
To Martius shall be honors, though indeed
In aught he merit not.

SICINIUS   Let's hence and hear
How the dispatch is made and in what fashion,   260
More than his singularity, he goes
Upon this present action.

BRUTUS   Let's along.   *Exeunt.*

---

241. **The present wars devour him**: They hope he is killed in the war. 243-44. **Tickled with good success**: flattered, heady with success. —**shadow...noon**: Martius sees himself as a god, who at the height of success, like someone in the noon-day sun, casts no shadow. See also 4.2.35, 4.5.97, 4.5.112, 4.5.181, 4.6.90, 4.6.100, 5.1.33, 5.3.184. 245-46. **commanded/ Under Cominius**: See 1.1.220, above. —**Fame, at the which he aims**: The charge that Coriolanus does not serve Rome is often repeated and, until his final capitulation, proves to be true. 249-51. **for what miscarries...giddy censure**: The tribunes argue that Martius has only deferred command so that, if anything goes wrong, his personal reputation/ war record will not be besmirched; another sign that these tribunes think more about politics than the good of Rome. Nonetheless, their analysis seems to be correct. See 1.4.29-30, in which Martius oversteps his command and gives orders directly to the men. 260. **How the dispatch is made and in what fashion**: How and in what fashion the troops will be led. 261. **singularity**: How Martius is or may be singled out for praise or special honor.

SCENE II. [*Corioles. The Senate House.*]

Enter Tullus Aufidius with Senators of Corioles.

1 SENATOR So, your opinion is, Aufidius,
That they of Rome are ent'red in our counsels
And know how we proceed.

AUFIDIUS   Is it not yours?
What ever have been thought on in this state
That could be brought to bodily act ere Rome   5
Had circumvention? 'Tis not four days gone
Since I heard thence. These are the words. I think
I have the letter here. Yes, here it is:
"They have press'd a power, but it is not known
Whether for east or west. The dearth is great,   10
The people mutinous; and it is rumor'd,
Cominius, Martius your old enemy
(Who is of Rome worse hated than of you),
And Titus Lartius, a most valiant Roman,
These three lead on this preparation   15
Whither 'tis bent. Most likely 'tis for you.
Consider of it."

1 SENATOR   Our army's in the field.
We never yet made doubt but Rome was ready
To answer us.

AUFIDIUS   Nor did you think it folly
To keep your great pretences veil'd till when   20
They needs must show themselves, which in the hatching,

SCENE II

2. **ent'red in our counsels**: aware of our meetings and apparently aware that they have a spy in their midst. Martius does have inside information (1.1.210-12); perhaps the old man, mentioned at 1.9.81-82, is his informant. 6. **circumvention**: news, information; Rome is always one step ahead. 7. **Since I heard thence**: Aufidius also has a spy in Rome; a sign that he, like Martius, is a warrior and intelligence officer. 9. **press'd a power**: raised an army. 10. **dearth**: famine. 13. **worse hated than of you**: Martius even beats out Aufidius as No. 1 Enemy of the People of Rome; a foreshadowing that the people will eventually turn on Martius. 16. **bent**: aimed, like a bow readied with an arrow.

It seem'd, appear'd to Rome. By the discovery
We shall be short'ned in our aim, which was
To take in many towns ere (almost) Rome
Should know we were afoot.

2 SENATOR   Noble Aufidius,   25
Take your commission; hie you to your bands.
Let us alone to guard Corioles.
If they set down before 's, for the remove
Bring up your army; but, I think, you'll find
Th' have not prepar'd for us.

AUFIDIUS   O, doubt not that!   30
I speak from certainties. Nay more,
Some parcels of their power are forth already
And only hitherward. I leave your honors.
If we and Caius Martius chance to meet,
'Tis sworn between us we shall ever strike   35
Till one can do no more.

ALL   The gods assist you!

AUFIDIUS   And keep your honors safe!

1 SENATOR   Farewell.

2 SENATOR   Farewell.

ALL   Farewell.

Exeunt omnes.

SCENE III. [*Rome. A room in the house of* Martius.]

Enter Volumnia and Virgilia, mother and wife to Martius.
They set them down on two low stools and sew.†

22-25. **By the discovery…we were afoot**: The idea was to surprise Rome and capture many of the outlying towns before the Romans could raise an army; "taken in" may also be read as take in allies. Rome was, after all, not a country but a city-state, and other cities under Roman power paid tribute to Rome without necessarily enjoying the rights of being a Roman citizen. Thus, as happened in the Second Punic War (218 BC – 201 BC), many city-states, tired of paying Roman tribute, defected to the side of Carthage. 28. **for the remove**: For the removal of the Roman army, in case it attacks.
32. **parcels of their power**: A part, a small unit, a scout party. 36. **no more**: fight no more; till one of them surrender or die in combat.

†   How to stage this domestic scene? The 1984 BBC TV version (dir Elijah Moshinsky) looks like it was set in seventeenth-century Holland; this particular scene looks like a Johan Vermeer painting, a domestic setting framed by a careful interplay of light and shade.

Volumnia and Virgilia mime sewing, a traditional pastime of Roman women awaiting their warring husbands. The effect of the miming is here oddly cold and mechanical (Steven Berkoff's *Coriolanus*, Globe Theatre, Tokyo, 1997.

VOLUMNIA   I pray you, daughter, sing, or express yourself in a more comfortable sort. If my son were my husband, I should freelier rejoice in that absence wherein he won honor than in the embracements of his bed where he would show most love. When yet he was but tender-bodied and the only son of my womb, when youth with comeliness pluck'd all gaze his way, when for a day of kings' entreaties a mother should not sell him an hour from her beholding, I (considering how honor would become such a person; that it was no better than picture-like to hang by th' wall, if renown made it not stir) was pleas'd to let him seek danger where he was like to find fame. To a cruel war I sent him, from whence he return'd, his brows bound with oak. I tell thee, daughter, I sprang not more in joy at first hearing he was a man-child than now in first seeing he had proved himself a man.   15

VIRGILIA   But had he died in the business, madam, how then?

SCENE III
2. **If my son were my husband**: Of course, we never hear of Volumnia's husband, but clearly the line reveals the strong bond she feels with Martius. It also suggests that Martius' interest in honor—earned in this society by deeds in war—was instilled by his mother at a very early age. When other mothers protected their sons, she sent him to fight. See also 1.3.2, 2.1.177-81, 3.2.108, 4.1.20. 6-7. **all gaze his way**: Martius was a pretty boy, girlish. See 2.2.87. 13. **his brows bound with oak**: A garland of oak leaves, worn at Roman "triumphs," ceremonies honoring great deeds of battle.

| VOLUMNIA | Then his good report should have been my son; I therein would have found issue. Hear me profess sincerely, had I a dozen sons, each in my love alike, and none less dear than thine and my good Martius, I had rather had eleven die   20 nobly for their country than one voluptuously surfeit out of action.† |

Enter a Gentlewoman.

GENTLEWOMAN	Madam, the Lady Valeria is come to visit you.
VIRGILIA	Beseech you give me leave to retire myself.
VOLUMNIA	Indeed you shall not. 25 Methinks I hear hither your husband's drum; See him pluck Aufidius down by th' hair; As children from a bear, the Volsces shunning him. Methinks I see him stamp thus, and call thus: "Come on, you cowards! You were got in fear, 30 Though you were born in Rome." His bloody brow With his mail'd hand then wiping, forth he goes, Like to a harvestman that's task'd to mow Or all or lose his hire.
VIRGILIA	His bloody brow? O Jupiter, no blood! 35
VOLUMNIA	Away, you fool! It more becomes a man Than gilt his trophy. The breasts of Hecuba When she did suckle Hector, look'd not lovelier Than Hector's forehead when it spit forth blood At Grecian sword, contemning. Tell Valeria 40 We are fit to bid her welcome. *Exit Gentlewoman.*

---

17. **Then his good report should have been my son**: Volumnia would rather her son die bravely in battle than live a long and comfortable, but unexceptional, life. In many ways she has raised her son as another Achilles, the great Greek warrior of the Trojan War, who had the choice of either a short but glorious or long but anonymous existence. 21-22. **surfeit out of action**: an overindulgent life without the threat of violence, and thus, without the chance of gaining Roman honor. 24. **leave to retire myself**: Virgilia believes that her role is to remain solitary or, if seen, to show constant signs of anxiety for her husband's safety. The older and more experienced Valeria shows far less anxiety. She has been through this before. 29-33. **Methinks I hear.... task'd to mow**: Volumnia imagines herself by Martius' side, reveling with her son in exploits of blood spilling. 36. **more becomes a man**: The question here is, does it become the woman? However, neither Virgilia nor Valeria display the sheer exuberance of Volumnia, who sees herself as a would-be woman warrior, kept from the wars by her gender. She, nonetheless, repeatedly flouts her gender role. See 1.3.69 and 2.1.105, below. 37-40. **The breasts of Hecuba...spit forth blood/ At Grecian sword**: A bizarre telescoping of the Trojan War. In her retelling, Hector, son of Hecuba, is breast fed and, within three lines, killed by Achilles' sword. The beauty of the breast, aching with mother's milk, and the splitting of the child's skull suggest a deep-seated hatred of her own sexuality and a longing to project that violence against her son. 41. **fit**: ready.

---

† 　 Volumnia's masculine desire: For his 2009 Olde Globe production, director Tresnjak intermingled an exchange between Volumnia (Celeste Ciulla) and Coriolanus' wife, Virgilia (Brooke Novak), with glimpses from battle scenes, which Volumnia, in her mind's eye, watches "with an almost leering pride and possessiveness"(James Hebert, *Union Tribune*, July 6, 2009).

VIRGILIA	Heavens bless my lord from fell Aufidius!
VOLUMNIA	He'll beat Aufidius' head below his knee And tread upon his neck.

Enter Valeria (with an Usher) and a Gentlewoman.

VALERIA	My ladies both, good day to you.	45
VOLUMNIA	Sweet madam!	
VIRGILIA	I am glad to see your ladyship.	
VALERIA	How do you both? You are manifest housekeepers. What are you sewing here? A fine spot, in good faith. How does your little son?	50
VIRGILIA	I thank your ladyship; well, good madam.	
VOLUMNIA	He had rather see the swords and hear a drum than look upon his schoolmaster.	
VALERIA	O' my word, the father's son! I'll swear 'tis a very pretty boy. O' my troth, I look'd upon him a Wednesday half an hour together. Has such a confirm'd countenance! I saw him run after a gilded butterfly; and when he caught it, he let it go again, and after it again, and over and over he comes, and up again; catch'd it again; or whether his fall enrag'd him or how 'twas, he did so set his teeth and tear it! O, I warrant, how he mammock'd it!†	55 60
VOLUMNIA	One on 's father's moods.	
VALERIA	Indeed, la, 'tis a noble child.	
VIRGILIA	A crack, madam.	
VALERIA	Come, lay aside your stitchery. I must have you play the idle housewife with me this afternoon.	66

42. **fell**: deadly. 48. **housekeepers**: Staying within the house, doing domestic chores; this is said approvingly and we must infer that this is the traditional role of women in war or in time of their men's absence. Recall that in the *Odyssey*, Penelope, awaiting her husband Odysseus, passes the years in near-solitary self-confinement, weaving a tapestry. See also line 78, below, which compares Virgilia directly to Penelope. 52. **see the swords and hear a drum**: Naturally, Volumnia is already instilling the same "virtues" that molded young Martius. See next line: "the father's son." 57-60. **gilded butterfly...set his teeth and tear it**: To my mind, destroying such a beautiful and defenseless creature is a sign of mental illness, but approved of in militant and ultraviolent Rome. 61. **mammock'd**: tore it to pieces. 62. **father's moods**: See commentary at line 2, above. 64. **crack**: A chip off the same block. Another Martius.

---

†   Reacting against patriarchal norms: At Valeria's recount of her sons exploits, Virgilia (Brooke Novak) was horrified (Olde Globe, San Diego, 2009; dir. Darko Tresnjak). In Steven Berkoff's 1991 production, Valeria was excised and the lines were given to Virgilia, who, as a consequence, was a much darker figure.

VIRGILIA	No, good madam. I will not out of doors.
VALERIA	Not out of doors?
VOLUMNIA	She shall, she shall!
VIRGILIA	Indeed, no, by your patience. I'll not over the threshold till my lord return from the wars. 71
VALERIA	Fie, you confine yourself most unreasonably. Come, you must go visit the good lady that lies in.
VIRGILIA	I will wish her speedy strength and visit her with my prayers, but I cannot go thither. 75
VOLUMNIA	Why, I pray you?
VIRGILIA	'Tis not to save labor nor that I want love.
VALERIA	You would be another Penelope. Yet, they say, all the yarn she spun in Ulysses' absence did but fill Ithaca full of moths. Come, I would your cambric were sensible as your finger, that you might leave pricking it for pity. Come, you shall go 81 with us.
VIRGILIA	No, good madam, pardon me. Indeed I will not forth.
VALERIA	In truth, la, go with me, and I'll tell you excellent news of your husband. 85
VIRGILIA	O, good madam, there can be none yet.
VALERIA	Verily I do not jest with you. There came news from him last night.
VIRGILIA	Indeed, madam?
VALERIA	In earnest, it's true; I heard a senator speak it. Thus it is: the 90 Volsces have an army forth; against whom Cominius the general is gone with one part of our Roman power. Your lord and Titus Lartius are set down before their city Corioles. They nothing doubt prevailing and to make it brief wars. This is true, on mine honor; and so I pray go with us. 95
VIRGILIA	Give me excuse, good madam. I will obey you in everything hereafter.

---

69. **She shall**: Unsurprisingly, the masculine Volumnia objects to Virgilia's traditional and gender-appropriate behavior. See 1.3.2. 73. **lies in**: about to give birth. 74. **speedy strength**: a quick delivery. 77. **not to save labor nor that I want love**: Punning on labor pains; Virgilia is not too lazy (the labor of the walk) to see the woman in labor. 79. **moths**: Valeria also makes light of traditional Roman duties; the tone here, however, suggests that she is trying to relieve, rather than dismiss, Virgilia's anxiety. 80. **cambric**: fine linen, associated with northeastern France. 81. **pricking**: sewing. 93-94. **set down... brief wars**: The army waits; presumably, they expect Corioli to surrender without a fight. 96-97. **I will obey you in everything hereafter**: Politely, Virgilia restates that she will not go until she is sure her husband is safe.

VOLUMNIA	Let her alone, lady. As she is now, she will but disease our better mirth.
VALERIA	In troth, I think she would.—Fare you well then.—Come, good sweet lady.—Prithee, Virgilia, turn thy solemness out o' door and go along with us. 102
VIRGILIA	No, at a word, madam. Indeed I must not. I wish you much mirth.
VALERIA	Well then, farewell. *Exeunt Ladies.* 105

SCENE IV. [*Before Corioles.*]

Enter Martius, Titus Lartius, with Drum and Colors, with Captains and Soldiers, as before the city Corioles: to them a Messenger.

MARTIUS	Yonder comes news. A wager they have met.
LARTIUS	My horse to yours, no.†
MARTIUS	'Tis done.
LARTIUS	Agreed.
MARTIUS	Say, has our general met the enemy?
MESSENGER	They lie in view, but have not spoke as yet.
LARTIUS	So, the good horse is mine.
MARTIUS	I'll buy him of you. 5
LARTIUS	No, I'll nor sell nor give him. Lend you him I will For half a hundred years. Summon the town.
MARTIUS	How far off lie these armies?
MESSENGER	Within this mile and half.
MARTIUS	Then shall we hear their 'larum and they ours. 10

98. **disease**: ruin, affect. See similar images at 1.3.98, 1.4.31-33, 3.1.77-79, 3.1.153-60, 3.1.219-20, 3.1.294-95, 3.2.33, 3.3.121-22, 4.2.11, 4.6.76. 101-02. **turn thy solemness out o'doors**: Solemn and indoors, turned inside out with her leaving the house; in short, cheer up and come with us. 104. **mirth**: fun.

SCENE IV
1. **Yonder comes**: Here comes.—**met**: met in battle. 4. **spoke as yet**: The report or sound of cannon. Rome had no cannons, but then again, Romans didn't speak English either, nor did Roman women stitch cambric. See 1.3.80, above. 5. **buy him of you**: The easy banter again suggests that Martius can be very obliging when dealing with his own class. 7. **Summon the town**: Summon the governor of the town for a parley. See line 12.*sd.*, below. 10. **'larum**: War drums and the clash of battle.

† Martius' horse: Director Steven Berkoff (Munich, 1991) had the company mime the act of riding stallions by "rising slowly and majestically up and down" (Steven Berkoff, *Coriolanus in Deutschland* [London: Amber Lane Press, 1992. 36]).

Now, Mars, I prithee make us quick in work,
That we with smoking swords may march from hence
To help our fielded friends! Come, blow thy blast.

They sound a parley. Enter two Senators with others on the walls of Corioles.

Tullus Aufidius, is he within your walls?

1 SENATOR   No, nor a man that fears you less than he.   15
That's lesser than a little.   *Drum afar off.*
                             Hark, our drums
Are bringing forth our youth! We'll break our walls
Rather than they shall pound us up. Our gates,
Which yet seem shut, we have but pinn'd with rushes;
They'll open of themselves.   *Alarum far off.*
                      Hark you, far off!   20
There is Aufidius. List what work he makes
Amongst your cloven army.

MARTIUS   O, they are at it!

LARTIUS   Their noise be our instruction. Ladders, ho!

Enter the Army of the Volsces.

MARTIUS   They fear us not, but issue forth their city.
Now put your shields before your hearts, and fight   25
With hearts more proof than shields. Advance, brave Titus.
They do disdain us much beyond our thoughts,
Which makes me sweat with wrath. Come on, my fellows.
He that retires, I'll take him for a Volsce,
And he shall feel mine edge.   30

Alarum. The Romans are beat back to their trenches. Enter Martius, cursing.

MARTIUS   All the contagion of the South light on you,
You shames of Rome! you herd of—Biles and plagues

---

11. **Mars**: God of War. 12. **smoking swords**: The steam of hot blood, thus smoking. 13. **fielded**: in the field of battle. 13.*sd.* **sound a parley**: a temporary truce. 14. **within your walls**: within the city. 15-16. **nor a man that fears you...lesser than a little**: In other words, neither Aufidius nor we are afraid of you. 16. **drums**: war drums. 17. **youth**: army, vital and exuberant, thus youthful. 18. **pound us up**: Think dog pound, i.e. locked up like animals. 19. **pinn'd with rushes**: Kept together with bulrushes, easily opened. 21. **List what work**: Listen to how he is killing Roman soldiers. 22. **cloven**: cut in two. Aufidius is cutting through the heart of the Roman army. **—they are at it**: At battle, but the language also suggest a sexual excitement; "at it"—fornicating. This mixture of sex and war is common in the speech of Martius *and* Aufidius. See 1.1.215. 23. **Ladders**: Used in siege warfare. 25-26. **shields... hearts...hearts...shields**: May your shields protect your heart and make you brave. 27. **beyond our thoughts**: More than we could have imagined possible. 28. **sweat with wrath**: eager to punish them. 29. **retires**: retreats. 30. **mine edge**: edge of my sword. Martius will kill any of his own men that retreat. Note that once the war begins, he seems to be firmly in charge; Titus Lartius is completely silent. 31. **contagion**: diseases. See 1.3.98. 31. **South**: Damp and, therefore, thought to be disease-ridden. 32. **Biles**: boils, a symptom of the plague.

Plaster you o'er, that you may be abhorr'd
Farther than seen and one infect another
Against the wind a mile! You souls of geese   35
That bear the shapes of men, how have you run
From slaves that apes would beat! Pluto and hell!
All hurt behind! backs red, and faces pale
With flight and agued fear! Mend and charge home,
Or, by the fires of heaven, I'll leave the foe   40
And make my wars on you! Look to't. Come on!
If you'll stand fast, we'll beat them to their wives,
As they us to our trenches. Follow me!

Another alarum. [The Volsces retire,] and Martius follows them to gates, and is shut in.

So, now the gates are ope.† Now prove good seconds.
'Tis for the followers fortune widens them,   45
Not for the fliers. Mark me and do the like.   *Enter the gates.*

1 SOLDIER   Foolhardiness! Not I.

2 SOLDIER   Nor I.

1 SOLDIER   See, they have shut him in.   *Alarum continues.*

ALL   To th' pot, I warrant him.

Enter Titus Lartius.

LARTIUS   What is become of Martius?

ALL   Slain, sir, doubtless.

1 SOLDIER   Following the fliers at the very heels,   50
With them he enters; who upon the sudden
Clapp'd to their gates. He is himself alone,
To answer all the city.

---

33. **Plaster you o'er**: A common cure for plague; mallow or a *plaster* was used to ripen the boil and to draw out the pus therein. 35. **souls of geese**: cowards who fly away. 37. **apes**: Subhumans. See 1.1.145, in which Martius calls the enlisted men of Rome rats. 37. **Pluto**: God of the Underworld. 39. **Mend and charge home**: Improve and charge forward toward the enemy. 41. **make my wars on you**: attack his own army. A repeated threat. See 1.4.29-30. 42. **we'll beat them to their wives**: We'll beat them until they run home. 44. **seconds**: backup. 45-46. **fortune widens them,/Not for the fliers**: Similar to our own expression, "fortune favors the brave." 46. **Mark me**: watch and copy me. 48. **shut him in**: Martius has rushed into the city alone; and the gates have now closed in, locking him in the walls of Corioli. The soldiers' cowardice/common sense may suggest that they are enlisted men, the very same Martius has repeatedly insulted and devalued. 49. **Slain**: killed. 50. **fliers**: The Volsces in retreat. 52. **Clapp'd**: shut.

---

†   Staging the battle: Director Steven Berkoff (Munich, 1991) had the company stylize the action by adding slow-motion, cinematic movements (Steven Berkoff, *Coriolanus in Deutschland*, 45). At Corioli, for example, Martius and his men "put their shoulders against an invisible obstacle"; Berkoff then casually remarked, "The gates are open," and strolled into the city (Irving Wardle, *The Independent on Sunday*, May 21, 1995).

LARTIUS   O noble fellow!
Who sensibly outdares his senseless sword
And when it bows, stand'st up! Thou art lost, Martius.   55
A carbuncle entire, as big as thou art,
Were not so rich a jewel. Thou wast a soldier
Even to Cato's wish, not fierce and terrible
Only in strokes, but with thy grim looks and
The thunder-like percussion of thy sounds   60
Thou mad'st thine enemies shake, as if the world
Were feverous and did tremble.

Enter Martius, bleeding, assaulted by the Enemy.

1 SOLDIER   Look, sir.

LARTIUS   O, 'tis Martius!
Let's fetch him off or make remain alike.
                          They fight, and all enter the city.

SCENE V. *[Corioles. A street.]*

Enter certain Romans with spoils.

1 ROMAN   This will I carry to Rome.

2 ROMAN   And I this.

3 ROMAN   A murrain on't! I took this for silver.

Alarum continues still afar off.

Enter Martius and Titus [Lartius] with a Trumpet.

MARTIUS   See here these movers that do prize their honors
At a crack'd drachma! Cushions, leaden spoons,   5
Irons of a doit, doublets that hangmen would
Bury with those that wore them, these base slaves,
Ere yet the fight be done, pack up. Down with them!
                          Exeunt [the Spoilers].
And hark, what noise the general makes! To him!

---

54. **senseless sword**: Difficult. Perhaps brave fighting spirit? 56-57. **carbuncle...jewel**: priceless, thus, a costly lost. 58. **Cato's wish**: Cato lived his life with a strict moral code. —**fierce and terrible...did tremble**: Roughly, you were so powerful and feared, the very earth trembled when you were angry or violent. 63. **fetch him off**: save him from the enemy; aid him.
SCENE V
1. **This**: Presumably treasure, spoils of war. 3. **murrain**: a sickness, common to cattle. 4-8. **movers... pack up**: The soldiers, who did not even fight bravely, are, in Martius' view, too quick to start scavenging for valuables. The battle is not yet over. 9. **noise**: the sound of battle.

	There is the man of my soul's hate, Aufidius,	10
	Piercing our Romans. Thou, valiant Titus, take	
	Convenient numbers to make good the city,	
	Whilst I, with those that have the spirit, will haste	
	To help Cominius.	

LARTIUS   Worthy sir, thou bleed'st.
Thy exercise hath been too violent for   15
A second course of fight.

MARTIUS   Sir, praise me not.
My work hath yet not warm'd me. Fare you well.
The blood I drop is rather physical
Than dangerous to me. To Aufidius thus
I will appear and fight.

LARTIUS   Now the fair goddess Fortune   20
Fall deep in love with thee, and her great charms
Misguide thy opposers' swords! Bold gentleman,
Prosperity be thy page!

MARTIUS   Thy friend no less
Than those she placeth highest! So farewell.

LARTIUS   Thou worthiest Martius!   [*Exit Martius.*] 25
Go sound thy trumpet in the market place.
Call thither all the officers o' th' town,
Where they shall know our mind. Away!
                    Exeunt.

SCENE VI. [*Near the camp of* Cominius.]

Enter Cominius as it were in retire, with Soldiers.

COMINIUS   Breathe you, my friends. Well fought! We are come off
Like Romans, neither foolish in our stands
Nor cowardly in retire. Believe me, sirs,

---

11. **Piercing**: cutting through, killing. 12. **to make good the city**: to secure the city. 15. **exercise**: fighting. 17. **yet not warm'd me**: I'm not even warmed up. 18. **physical**: good for me, healthful. 20. **appear**: appear all bloody and ready for combat. —**Fortune**: The goddess of chance. Lady Luck. 22. **Misguide the opposers' swords**: Protect you from the enemies' swords. 23-24. **page**: attendant, as in "Good luck be by your side." —**Thy friend no less/ Than those she placeth highest**: I am your friend as much as Fortune is my friend. 27. **thither**: here. 28. **our mind**: our intentions.

SCENE VI
Sd. as it were in retire: as if in retreat. 1. **Breathe you, my friends**: Relax. Note Cominius does not need to berate his soldiers to get the best out of them. —**We are come off**: We have acted. 2-3. **Like Romans,...in retire**: Even-tempered, prudent. By this measure, Coriolanus is unRoman.

We shall be charg'd again. Whiles we have struck,
By interims and conveying gusts we have heard   5
The charges of our friends. Ye Roman gods,
Lead their successes as we wish our own,
That both our powers, with smiling fronts encount'ring,
May give you thankful sacrifice!

Enter a Messenger.

Thy news?

MESSENGER   The citizens of Corioles have issued   10
And given to Lartius and to Martius battle.
I saw our party to their trenches driven,
And then I came away.

COMINIUS   Though thou speakest truth,
Methinks thou speak'st not well. How long is't since?

MESSENGER   Above an hour, my lord.   15

COMINIUS   'Tis not a mile; briefly we heard their drums.
How couldst thou in a mile confound an hour
And bring thy news so late?

MESSENGER   Spies of the Volsces
Held me in chase, that I was forc'd to wheel
Three or four miles about. Else had I, sir,   20
Half an hour since brought my report.

Enter Martius.

COMINIUS   Who's yonder
That does appear as he were flay'd? O gods!
He has the stamp of Martius, and I have
Beforetime seen him thus.

MARTIUS   Come I too late?†

---

4. **charg'd**: attacked. 5. **interims and conveying gusts**: Fought by turns, like the wind, sometimes changing in direction and intensity. 6-9. **our friends**: Other Romans, i.e. Titus Lartius and Martius. —**Ye Roman gods…sacrifice**: Roughly, May the Gods grant our armies victory over our enemies. 12-13. **trenches driven…came away**: Beaten back. The messenger came before Martius single-handedly stormed the town. 13-14. **truth…not well**: To speak the true should be to speak well, but your truth is nothing but bad news. 18. **news so late**: It took an hour for the messenger to travel a mile.
19. **Held me in chase**: Chased him, forced him to detour, thus delaying his arrival. The information suggests the perilous nature of the battle. 22. **flay'd**: Martius looks like raw meat, beaten and bloody. 24. **Beforetime seen him thus**: Clearly, Martius always fights like a madman. 24. **Come I too late**: Martius is spoiling for a fight with Aufidus.

---

†   The battle at Corioli: Ian McKellen (London's Nation Theatre, 1985; dir. Peter Hall) entered "near naked streaming with blood" (Jack Kroll, "The Grand Style: In London. Three great actors go for broke." *Newsweek*, January 7, 1985).

COMINIUS	The shepherd knows not thunder from a tabor	25
	More than I know the sound of Martius' tongue	
	From every meaner man.	

MARTIUS   Come I too late?

COMINIUS   Ay, if you come not in the blood of others,
            But mantled in your own.

MARTIUS   O, let me clip ye
            In arms as sound as when I woo'd, in heart   30
            As merry as when our nuptial day was done
            And tapers burn'd to bedward!

COMINIUS   Flower of warriors! How is't with Titus Lartius?

MARTIUS   As with a man busied about decrees:
            Condemning some to death, and some to exile;   35
            Ransoming him or pitying, threat'ning th' other;
            Holding Corioles in the name of Rome
            Even like a fawning greyhound in the leash,
            To let him slip at will.

COMINIUS   Where is that slave
            Which told me they had beat you to your trenches?   40
            Where is he? Call him hither.

MARTIUS   Let him alone.
            He did inform the truth. But for our gentlemen,
            The common file (a plague! tribunes for them!),
            The mouse ne'er shunn'd the cat as they did budge
            From rascals worse than they.

COMINIUS   But how prevail'd you?   45

MARTIUS   Will the time serve to tell? I do not think.
            Where is the enemy? Are you lords o' th' field?
            If not, why cease you till you are so?

29-31. **clip ye...woo'd...nuptial day**: Hug you, seduce you, have sex with you. Martius is passionate; a classic sadist. See commentary at 1.1.215. 33. **Flower of warriors**: As in "Flower of Chivalry"; the best of the best. 34. **busied about decrees**: Titus Lartius, as the newly-installed commander of the captured Corioli, is arresting and executing those he thinks most dangerous, and ransoming still others. 38-39. **fawning greyhound... let him slip at will**: A master who is firmly in command. —**slave**: fool. 43. **file**: rank and file, enlisted men. —**tribunes for them**: Martius objects to the common men having a say in the political destiny of the state, since they are, in his view, so cowardly. 44. **mouse... cat**: The enlisted men were like mice. 45. **worse than they**: Even more cowardly than the Roman soldiers. — **how prevail'd you**: Tell us how you conquered Corioli. Martius refuses; he's not interested in citing his own victories. A problem, as it turns out, when undergoing his confirmation for the post of Consul. See 2.3.41-46, below. 47. **lords o'th' field**: victors of the battle.

COMINIUS	Martius, we have at disadvantage fought,	
	And did retire to win our purpose.	50
MARTIUS	How lies their battle? Know you on which side	
	They have plac'd their men of trust?	
COMINIUS	As I guess, Martius,	
	Their bands i' th' vaward are the Antiates,	
	Of their best trust; o'er them Aufidius,	
	Their very heart of hope.	
MARTIUS	I do beseech you,	55
	By all the battles wherein we have fought,	
	By th' blood we have shed together, by th' vows	
	We have made to endure friends, that you directly	
	Set me against Aufidius and his Antiates;	
	And that you not delay the present, but,	60
	Filling the air with swords advanc'd and darts,	
	We prove this very hour.	
COMINIUS	Though I could wish	
	You were conducted to a gentle bath	
	And balms applied to you, yet dare I never	
	Deny your asking. Take your choice of those	65
	That best can aid your action.	
MARTIUS	Those are they	
	That most are willing. If any such be here	
	(As it were sin to doubt) that love this painting	
	Wherein you see me smear'd; if any fear	
	Lesser his person than an ill report;	70
	If any think brave death outweighs bad life	
	And that his country's dearer than himself,	
	Let him alone, or so many so minded,	
	Wave thus to express his disposition,	
	And follow Martius.	75

They all shout and wave their swords, take him up in
their arms and cast up their caps.

O, me alone? Make you a sword of me?

49-50. **disadvantage fought,/ And did retire to win**: While this sounds cowardly, Cominius describes a common battle technique, a rearguard movement. 52. **men of trust**: the best soldiers of the enemy. 53. **th'vaward**: vanguard. –**Antiates**: Presumably, the best of Aufidius' men, like Achilles' Myrmidons. 55-59. **I do beseech you... Aufidius**: I'm begging you, let me fight him. 60-61. **you not delay the present, but,/Filling the air with swords advanc'd and darts**: Let's draw our swords, fire our arrows, and advance on the enemy. 64. **balms**: healing ointments. 68. **painting**: blood. 70. **Lesser his person than an ill report**: In other words, to be called a coward. 75.*sd.* **cast up their caps**: The enlisted men did the same at 1.1.195; a sign that Martius can be a real leader of all of Rome under the right conditions. 76. **Make you a sword of me**: Martius wants to be aimed like a weapon.

If these shows be not outward, which of you
But is four Volsces? None of you but is
Able to bear against the great Aufidius
A shield as hard as his. A certain number   80
(Though thanks to all) must I select. The rest
Shall bear the business in some other fight,
As cause will be obey'd. Please you to march;
And I shall quickly draw out my command,
Which men are best inclin'd.

COMINIUS   March on, my fellows.   85
Make good this ostentation, and you shall
Divide in all with us.   *Exeunt.*

SCENE VII. [*The gates of Corioles.*]

*Titus Lartius, having set a guard upon Corioles, going with Drum
and Trumpet toward Cominius and Caius Martius, enters with
a Lieutenant, other Soldiers, and a Scout.*

LARTIUS   So, let the ports be guarded. Keep your duties
As I have set them down. If I do send, dispatch
Those centuries to our aid; the rest will serve
For a short holding. If we lose the field,
We cannot keep the town.

LIEUTENANT   Fear not our care, sir.   5

LARTIUS   Hence, and shut your gates upon's.
Our guider, come; to th' Roman camp conduct us. *Exeunt.*

SCENE VIII. [*A field of battle between the Roman and the Volscian camp.*]

Alarum, as in battle. Enter Martius and Aufidius at several doors.

MARTIUS   I'll fight with none but thee, for I do hate thee
Worse than a promise-breaker.

77-78. **which of you/But is four Volsces**: Any Roman soldier, he says, is worth four Volsces. 82. **bear the business**: fight elsewhere. 86-87. **ostentation...Divide in all**: Fight bravely and we'll split the booty with you; suggests that normally only the aristocratic leaders enjoy the spoils of war, contradicted by 1.5.4.
SCENE VII
1-5. **ports be guarded...cannot keep the town**: The military situation remains precarious. 7. **guider**: guide, scout.
SCENE VIII
1. **none but thee...I do hate**: Or respect as much as him; see 1.1.218-19.

The naked rage of Coriolanus (Steven Berkoff) encountering Tullus Aufidius (Colin McFarlane) in battle (*Coriolanus*, Globe Theatre, Tokyo, 1997).

AUFIDIUS   We hate alike.
            Not Afric owns a serpent I abhor
            More than thy fame and envy. Fix thy foot.

MARTIUS   Let the first budger die the other's slave,   5
            And the gods doom him after!

AUFIDIUS   If I fly, Martius,
            Holloa me like a hare.

MARTIUS   Within these three hours, Tullus,
            Alone I fought in your Corioles walls
            And made what work I pleas'd. 'Tis not my blood
            Wherein thou seest me mask'd. For thy revenge   10
            Wrench up thy power to th' highest.

AUFIDIUS   Wert thou the Hector
            That was the whip of your bragg'd progeny,
            Thou shouldst not scape me here.

            Here they fight, and certain Volsces come in the aid of Aufidius.
            Martius fights till they be driven in breathless.

---

3. **Not Afric owns a serpent I abhor**: In the Renaissance imagination, a place of monsters. 4. **fix thy foot**: Ready for battle. 5. **the first budger**: the first to move. 7. **hare**: Known for speed, but usually not the most ferocious of animals. A joke, perhaps? 9. **made what work I pleas'd**: killed who I wanted to kill; Aufidius can make a similar boast. Only Martius is his equal. 11-12. **Hector...progeny**: Hector won many battles against the Greeks. His relation, Aeneas, eventually founded a colony on the Italian peninsula. Thus, Romans are, technically, related to Hector. 13.*sd*. **certain Volsces come in the aid of Aufidius**: Since the fight is no longer *mano-a-mano*, Aufidius feels cheated.

Officious, and not valiant! you have sham'd me
In your condemned seconds.   [*Exeunt.*]   15

SCENE IX. [*The Roman camp.*]

Flourish. Alarum. A retreat is sounded. Enter, at one door, Cominius with the
Romans; at another door, Martius, with his arm in a scarf.

COMINIUS   If I should tell thee o'er this thy day's work,
Thou't not believe thy deeds; but I'll report it
Where senators shall mingle tears with smiles;
Where great patricians shall attend and shrug,
I' th' end admire; where ladies shall be frighted   5
And, gladly quak'd, hear more; where the dull tribunes,
That with the fusty plebeians hate thine honors,
Shall say, against their hearts, "We thank the gods
Our Rome hath such a soldier!"
Yet cam'st thou to a morsel of this feast,   10
Having fully din'd before.

Enter Titus [Lartius] with his Power, from the pursuit.

LARTIUS   O General,
Here is the steed, we the caparison.
Hadst thou beheld—

MARTIUS   Pray now, no more. My mother,
Who has a charter to extol her blood,
When she does praise me grieves me. I have done   15
As you have done—that's what I can; induc'd
As you have been—that's for my country.
He that has but effected his good will
Hath overta'en mine act.

COMINIUS   You shall not be
The grave of your deserving. Rome must know   20

---

15. **condemned seconds**: unwanted, thus condemnable, aid.
SCENE IX
Sd. arm in a scarf: bandaged. 2-3. **I'll report it/Where senators shall mingle tears with smiles**:
Evidence that Cominius believes that Martius has no issue discussing his feats with men of his own
class. Note that in line 4 Cominius expects the lower-class plebeians to admit Martius' worth, but he
fully expects the newly-made tribunes to privately scorn him. 12. **caparison**: decorative covering for a
horse; in short, Martius did all the real work. The rest of the army was merely for show. 14-20. **Who has
a charter...mine act**: A complicated way of saying that he's done only what family and country demand
of him, and what he demands of himself. **—You shall not be/The grave of your deserving**: You will
not bury/silence/kill the glory of your exploits.

The value of her own. 'Twere a concealment
Worse than a theft, no less than a traducement,
To hide your doings and to silence that
Which, to the spire and top of praises vouch'd,
Would seem but modest. Therefore, I beseech you   25
(In sign of what you are, not to reward
What you have done) before our army hear me.

MARTIUS   I have some wounds upon me, and they smart
To hear themselves rememb'red.

COMINIUS   Should they not,
Well might they fester 'gainst ingratitude   30
And tent themselves with death. Of all the horses
(Whereof we have ta'en good, and good store), of all
The treasure in this field achiev'd and city,
We render you the tenth, to be ta'en forth
Before the common distribution at   35
Your only choice.

MARTIUS   I thank you, General,
But cannot make my heart consent to take
A bribe to pay my sword. I do refuse it
And stand upon my common part with those
That have beheld the doing.   40

A long flourish. They all cry, "Martius! Martius!" cast up their caps and lances.
Cominius and Lartius stand bare.

May these same instruments which you profane
Never sound more! When drums and trumpets shall
I' th' field prove flatterers, let courts and cities be
Made all of false-fac'd soothing! When steel grows
Soft as the parasite's silk, let him be made   45
A coverture for th' wars! No more, I say!
For that I have not wash'd my nose that bled
Or foil'd some debile wretch (which without note

---

22. **theft, no less than a traducement**: Don't rob or slander yourself. 24. **spire and top**: comparing his deeds to a tower. 26. **sign...reward**: Take recognition not as a mercenary's reward, but as an acknowledgement of what was here accomplished. Contradicted by what follows at lines 29-36, in which Cominius offers him the first spoils of war; Martius turns him down. 28. **smart**: pain. 30. **fester**: infect. 38. **A bribe to pay my sword**: Martius doesn't kill for the money, but because it was asked and expected of him. What he does not acknowledge here is that he also enjoys the work. See 1.6.29-32.
42-45. **When drums and trumpets...When steel grows/ Soft**: Martius begins with a hopeful call for peace—"May these same instruments.../Never sound more"—but the rest of the speech praises the virtues of a regimented, disciplined, and, above all, militant society. Peace leads to softness and flattery.

Here's many else have done), you shout me forth
In acclamations hyperbolical,   50
As if I lov'd my little should be dieted
In praises sauc'd with lies.

COMINIUS   Too modest are you,
More cruel to your good report than grateful
To us that give you truly. By your patience,
If 'gainst yourself you be incens'd, we'll put you   55
(Like one that means his proper harm) in manacles,
Then reason safely with you. Therefore be it known,
As to us, to all the world, that Caius Martius
Wears this war's garland; in token of the which,
My noble steed, known to the camp, I give him   60
With all his trim belonging; and from this time,
For what he did before Corioles, call him,
With all th' applause and clamor of the host,
Caius Martius Coriolanus. Bear
Th' addition nobly ever!   65

Flourish. Trumpets sound and drums.

OMNES   Caius Martius Coriolanus!†

MARTIUS   I will go wash;
And when my face is fair, you shall perceive
Whether I blush or no. Howbeit, I thank you.
I mean to stride your steed, and at all times   70
To undercrest your good addition
To th' fairness of my power.

COMINIUS   So, to our tent,
Where, ere we do repose us, we will write
To Rome of our success. You, Titus Lartius,
Must to Corioles back. Send us to Rome   75

---

50. **acclamations hyperbolical**: Martius accuses his men of already falling for flattery. He may well be suggesting that his overwhelming victory is actually marking the end of an era, for without the Volsces, why does Rome need to retain her military virtues? Contradicted by Aufidius, who at 4.5.113 is already plotting another campaign. Ironically, the same idea is proposed by Volumnia at 5.3.138-140. 53. **more cruel to your good report**: To undervalue heroism is worse than to overvalue it. 55. **incens'd**: angry; if you fight against yourself. 56. **manacles**: As in, locked up like a madman. 59. **war's garland**: See 1.3.13, above. 60. **steed**: a warhorse for a warhorse. Horse trading is usually associated with bargaining, but, as we saw at 1.4.5, it is among these Romans seen as part of some complex, chivalric tradition. 64. **Coriolanus**: Honorary, because of his victory, but he is often still referred to as Martius. 69. **blush or no**: Since Martius is bloody, his blush is difficult to see. 71-72. **undercrest your good addition/To th' fairness of my power**: Try to live up to this new honor. 73. **repose**: sleep. 75. **Send us**: Send with us messages.

† Praising the hero: In the 1991 Munich production, the soldiers began chanting "Co-ri-o-la-nus" (Steven Berkoff, *Coriolanus in Deutschland*, 63).

	The best, with whom we may articulate	
	For their own good and ours.	

LARTIUS   I shall, my lord.

MARTIUS   The gods begin to mock me. I, that now
Refus'd most princely gifts, am bound to beg
Of my Lord General.

COMINIUS   Take't; 'tis yours. What is't?   80

MARTIUS   I sometime lay here in Corioles
At a poor man's house; he us'd me kindly.
He cried to me; I saw him prisoner;
But then Aufidius was within my view,
And wrath o'erwhelm'd my pity. I request you   85
To give my poor host freedom.

COMINIUS   O, well begg'd!
Were he the butcher of my son, he should
Be free as is the wind. Deliver him, Titus.

LARTIUS   Martius, his name?

MARTIUS   By Jupiter, forgot!
I am weary; yea, my memory is tir'd.   90
Have we no wine here?

COMINIUS   Go we to our tent.
The blood upon your visage dries; 'tis time
It should be look'd to. Come.   *Exeunt.*

SCENE X. [*The camp of the Volsces.*]

A flourish. Cornets. Enter Tullus Aufidius bloody, with two or three Soldiers.

AUFIDIUS   The town is ta'en!

SOLDIER   'Twill be deliver'd back on good condition.

AUFIDIUS   Condition?

---

78. **The gods begin to mock me**: While Martius means this as a gentle jest, he is, ironically, correct, as, without knowing it, he is at the height of his career. 86. **poor host**: Perhaps the spy mentioned at 1.2.2-3. 89. **forgot**: That Martius has forgotten the man's name is curious. It might signal his sheer exhaustion from battle, or that his glories have catapulted him beyond his former life; renamed Coriolanus, he has forgotten or been still more distanced from the plebeians. But this is contradicted by (1.) the fact that Lartius continues to refer to him as Martius (1.9.89) and (2.) the fact that Martius still remembers the debt he owes the man. 92. **visage**: face.
SCENE X
2. **good condition**: ransomed back on good/easy terms.

I would I were a Roman; for I cannot,
Being a Volsce, be that I am. Condition?   5
What good condition can a treaty find
I' th' part that is at mercy? Five times, Martius,
I have fought with thee. So often hast thou beat me;
And wouldst do so, I think, should we encounter
As often as we eat. By th' elements,   10
If e'er again I meet him beard to beard,
He's mine, or I am his. Mine emulation
Hath not that honor in't it had; for where
I thought to crush him in an equal force,
True sword to sword, I'll potch at him some way.   15
Or wrath or craft may get him.

SOLDIER   He's the devil.

AUFIDIUS   Bolder, though not so subtle. My valor's poison'd
With only suff'ring stain by him; for him
Shall fly out of itself. Nor sleep nor sanctuary,
Being naked, sick, nor fane nor Capitol,   20
The prayers of priests nor times of sacrifice,
Embargements all of fury, shall lift up
Their rotten privilege and custom 'gainst
My hate to Martius. Where I find him, were it
At home, upon my brother's guard, even there,   25
Against the hospitable canon, would I
Wash my fierce hand in's heart. Go you to th' city.
Learn how 'tis held, and what they are that must
Be hostages for Rome.

SOLDIER   Will not you go?

AUFIDIUS   I am attended at the cypress grove. I pray you   30
('Tis south the city mills) bring me word thither
How the world goes, that to the pace of it
I may spur on my journey.

SOLDIER   I shall, sir.   [*Exeunt.*]

4-5. **I would I were a Roman;...that I am**: I want to be a winner, like the Romans. 10. **elements**: Gods.
11. **e'er**: ever. 11. **beard to beard**: face to face. 12. **emulation**: ambition. 15. **potch at him**: thrust,
wound him. 16. **Or wrath or craft**: by hook or by crook. 17-24. **subtle**: clever. –**valor's poison'd...
suff'ring stain...Shall fly out of itself**: My honor is stained/discolored; I hardly know myself. –**Nor
sleep...My hate**: A vow never to rest until Martius is dead. Ironically, his oath, made in defeat, echoes
Martius' speech, made in victory (1.9.40-44). Both prize the bloodlust of battle and the virtues of a
military life. 27. **hand in's heart**: Stab him in the heart. 30. **attended**: attended by counselors, no doubt
deep in negotiations with the Romans. 32. **How the world goes**: What news do you hear. 33. **spur on
my journey**: Use whatever information you can provide to hasten my revenge on Martius.

ACT II

SCENE I. [*Rome. A public place.*]

Enter Menenius, with the two Tribunes of the People, Sicinius and Brutus.

MENENIUS	The augurer tells me we shall have news tonight.
BRUTUS	Good or bad?
MENENIUS	Not according to the prayer of the people, for they love not Martius.
SICINIUS	Nature teaches beasts to know their friends. 5
MENENIUS	Pray you, who does the wolf love?
SICINIUS	The lamb.
MENENIUS	Ay, to devour him, as the hungry plebeians would the noble Martius.
BRUTUS	He's a lamb indeed, that bays like a bear. 10
MENENIUS	He's a bear indeed, that lives like a lamb. You two are old men. Tell me one thing I shall ask you.
BOTH	Well, sir.
MENENIUS	In what enormity is Martius poor in that you two have not in abundance? 15
BRUTUS	He's poor in no one fault, but stor'd with all.
SICINIUS	Especially in pride.
BRUTUS	And topping all others in boasting.
MENENIUS	This is strange now. Do you two know how you are censured here in the city, I mean of us o' th' right-hand file? Do you?
BOTH	Why, how are we censur'd? 21
MENENIUS	Because you talk of pride now—Will you not be angry?
BOTH	Well, well, sir, well.
MENENIUS	Why, 'tis no great matter, for a very little thief of occasion will rob you of a great deal of patience. 25

ACT II. SCENE I.
1. **augurer**: fortuneteller. 3-4. **they love not Martius**: The fortunetellers foresee a great victory for Martius. 5. **know their friends**: Of which, they infer, Martius is not. 8-9. **hungry plebeians would the noble Martius**: Menenius again speaks badly of the poor of Rome. See 1.1.184-86. 20. **right-hand file**: the aristocrats or patricians. 24. **'tis no great matter**: No great matter, whether they are insulted or not. Menenius shows aristocratic disdain for the tribunes.

	Give your dispositions the reins and be angry at your pleasures—at the least, if you take it as a pleasure to you in being so. You blame Martius for being proud.
BRUTUS	We do it not alone, sir.
MENENIUS	I know you can do very little alone; for your helps are many, or else your actions would grow wondrous single. Your abilities are too infant-like for doing much alone. You talk of pride. O that you could turn your eyes toward the napes of your necks and make but an interior survey of your good selves! O that you could! 35
BOTH	What then, sir?
MENENIUS	Why, then you should discover a brace of unmeriting, proud, violent, testy magistrates (alias fools) as any in Rome.
SICINIUS	Menenius, you are known well enough too.
MENENIUS	I am known to be a humorous patrician, and one that loves a cup of hot wine with not a drop of allaying Tiber in't; said to be something imperfect in favoring the first complaint, hasty and tinder-like upon too trivial motion; one that converses more with the buttock of the night than with the forehead of the morning. What I think, I utter, and spend my malice in my breath. Meeting two such wealsmen as you are (I cannot call you Lycurguses), if the drink you give me touch my palate adversely, I make a crooked face at it. I cannot say your worships have deliver'd the matter well when I find the ass in compound with the major part of your syllables; and though I must be content to bear with those that say you are reverend grave men, yet they lie deadly that tell you have good faces. If you see this in the map of my microcosm, follows it that I am known well enough too? What harm can your beesom conspectuities glean out of this character, if I be known well enough too? 56

---

26. **the reins and be angry**: Despite the fact that the tribunes in part control the state, it doesn't matter if they are angry; Menenius suggests that tribunes have created a sense of lawlessness in Rome. 32. **infant-like**: Menenius continues to insult the people's representatives. 33-34. **napes of your necks**: In other words, look at yourselves. 38. **testy**: quick to anger. 39. **well known enough too**: Interestingly, the tribunes do not contradict Menenius, but suggest that he too has faults. 41. **allaying Tiber**: I.e., no water in his wine. 44-45. **forehead of the morning**: given to partying all night. 46. **wealsmen**: politicians, possibly combining weasels and wisemen. Ironic. 47. **Lycurguses**: After Lycurgus, the lawgiver of Greece. 47-48. **drink...crooked face at it**: To make a sour face after drinking sour wine. Not one to hide the truth. A plain speaker. 49-52. **ass in compound...good faces**: Ironic. Supposedly honest men who act as asses. 54-55. **beesom conspectuities**: Perhaps "beseeming conspicuousness."

BRUTUS   Come, sir, come, we know you well enough.

MENENIUS   You know neither me, yourselves, nor anything. You are
                    ambitious for poor knaves' caps and legs. You wear out
                    a good wholesome forenoon in hearing a cause between
                    an orange-wife and a forset-seller, and then rejourn the
                    controversy of threepence to a second day of audience. When
                    you are hearing a matter between party and party, if you
                    chance to be pinch'd with the colic, you make faces like
                    mummers, set up the bloody flag against all patience, and, in
                    roaring for a chamber pot, dismiss the controversy bleeding,
                    the more entangled by your hearing. All the peace you make
                    in their cause is, calling both the parties knaves. You are a
                    pair of strange ones.

BRUTUS   Come, come, you are well understood to be a perfecter giber
                    for the table than a necessary bencher in the Capitol.   71

MENENIUS   Our very priests must become mockers if they shall
                    encounter such ridiculous subjects as you are. When you
                    speak best unto the purpose, it is not worth the wagging of
                    your beards; and your beards deserve not so honorable a grave
                    as to stuff a botcher's cushion or to be entomb'd in an ass's
                    packsaddle. Yet you must be saying Martius is proud; who,
                    in a cheap estimation, is worth all your predecessors since
                    Deucalion, though peradventure some of the best of 'em were
                    hereditary hangmen. God-den to your worships. More of
                    your conversation would infect my brain, being the herdsmen
                    of the beastly plebeians. I will be bold to take my leave of
                    you.   83

                              Brutus and Sicinius aside.

                    Enter Volumnia, Virgilia, and Valeria.

                    How now, my as fair as noble ladies—and the moon, were
                    she earthly, no nobler, whither do you follow your eyes so
                    fast?   86

61-62. **orange-wife...second day**: Waste hours on trivial matters but think yourselves all important.
66. **chamber pot**: A pot to piss in. 68. **knaves**: Fools, or, in this case, fools calling fools fools. 70-71.
perfecter giber for the table than a necessary bencher: Given to eating and to drinking more than
to adjudicating a serious matter in the courts of law. 74-75. **wagging of your beards**: Your "wisdom" is
not worth the movement of your mouths. 76. **botcher's cushion...ass's packsaddle**: Your beards might
as well stuff cushions or saddles. Insulting their age/reverence/wisdom. 79. **Deucalion**: The Greek gods
wiped out man with a flood, except for Deucalion and his wife Pyrrha, who, like Noah and Na'amah,
were saved. 80. **hereditary hangmen**: habitual criminals, lowlives. 81-82. **herdsmen of the beastly**:
Leaders of the pack, playing upon wolf and lamb in lines 5-9, above. 84. **fair...noble...moon**: White
as the moon, spotless, sinless. 86. **fast**: quickly.

VOLUMNIA	Honorable Menenius, my boy Martius approaches. For the love of Juno, let's go.
MENENIUS	Ha? Martius coming home?
VOLUMNIA	Ay, worthy Menenius, and with most prosperous approbation. 90
MENENIUS	Take my cap, Jupiter, and I thank thee. Hoo! Martius coming home?
2 LADIES	Nay, 'tis true.
VOLUMNIA	Look, here's a letter from him. The state hath another, his 95 wife another, and, I think, there's one at home for you.
MENENIUS	I will make my very house reel tonight. A letter for me?
VIRGILIA	Yes, certain, there's a letter for you. I saw't.
MENENIUS	A letter for me? It gives me an estate of seven years' health, in which time I will make a lip at the physician. The most 100 sovereign prescription in Galen is but empiricutic and, to this preservative, of no better report than a horse-drench. Is he not wounded? He was wont to come home wounded.
VIRGILIA	O, no, no, no!
VOLUMNIA	O, he is wounded! I thank the gods for't. 105
MENENIUS	So do I too, if it be not too much. Brings 'a victory in his pocket? The wounds become him.
VOLUMNIA	On's brows. Menenius, he comes the third time home with the oaken garland.
MENENIUS	Has he disciplin'd Aufidius soundly? 110
VOLUMNIA	Titus Lartius writes they fought together, but Aufidius got off.
MENENIUS	And 'twas time for him too, I'll warrant him that. An he had stay'd by him, I would not have been so fidius'd for all the chests in Corioles and the gold that's in them. Is the Senate possess'd of this? 116

88. **Juno**: Zeus' wife and protectress of Rome. 90-91. **prosperous approbation**: With a hero's welcome. 97. **reel**: shake with dancing, celebration. 99. **estate of seven years' health**: In other words, a new lease on life. 101-102. **Galen is but empiricutic...a horse-drench**: Galen, a famous doctor, is a mere horse doctor compared to this good news. 105. **he is wounded**: Volumnia's happiness here suggests the virtue of wounds and battlescars. 107. **pocket**: stored safely. As in "pocket my winnings." 109. **oaken garland**: A hero's welcome. See 1.3.13. 110. **disciplin'd**: beaten. 111-112. **got off**: survived. 114-115. **fidius'd for all the chests in Corioles**: I would not be beaten like Aufidius for all the gold in Corioles. 116. **possess'd**: informed.

VOLUMNIA	Good ladies, let's go. Yes, yes, yes! The Senate has letters from the General, wherein he gives my son the whole name of the war. He hath in this action outdone his former deeds doubly.
VALERIA	In troth, there's wondrous things spoke of him. 120
MENENIUS	Wondrous? Ay, I warrant you, and not without his true purchasing.
VIRGILIA	The gods grant them true!
VOLUMNIA	True? Pow, waw!
MENENIUS	True? I'll be sworn they are true. Where is he wounded? 125 [*To the Tribunes*] God save your good worships! Martius is coming home. He has more cause to be proud.—Where is he wounded?
VOLUMNIA	I' th' shoulder and i' th' left arm. There will be large cicatrices to show the people when he shall stand for his 130 place. He received in the repulse of Tarquin seven hurts i' th' body.
MENENIUS	One i' th' neck, and two i' th' thigh. There's nine that I know.
VOLUMNIA	He had before this last expedition twenty-five wounds upon him.
MENENIUS	Now it's twenty-seven. Every gash was an enemy's grave. (*A shout and flourish.*) Hark! the trumpets.
VOLUMNIA	These are the ushers of Martius. Before him he carries noise, and behind him he leaves tears. 140 Death, that dark spirit, in's nervy arm doth lie, Which, being advanc'd, declines, and then men die.

A sennet. Trumpets sound. Enter Cominius the General and Titus Lartius;
between them, Martius, crown'd with an oaken garland;
with Captains and Soldiers and a Herald.

---

118. **whole name**: All the credit. 121-22. **true purchasing**: He paid for his deeds in action. 124. **Pow, waw**: Psha, of course! 130. **cicatrices**: scars. 131. **Tarquin**: Former King of Rome, overthrown in favor of a governmental aristocracy, in which a few of the most prominent citizens rule. That Martius favors aristocracy over full democracy is well expressed throughout 1.1, though, given his autocratic behavior, it is ironic that he fought against Tarquin. 134-35. **There's nine...twenty-five**: Like Volumnia, Menenius is thrilled that Martius has been repeatedly wounded. 139-40. **noise...tears**: a noise of victory in the wake of mourners, who cry over the dead he leaves behind him. Ironic, in that Volumnia will be left to mourn the death of her own child. 141. **nervy**: muscled.

HERALD	Know, Rome, that all alone Martius did fight
	Within Corioles gates, where he hath won,
	With fame, a name to Caius Martius. These 145
	In honor follows Coriolanus. Welcome,
	Welcome to Rome, renowned Coriolanus! *Sound. Flourish.*
ALL	Welcome to Rome, renowned Coriolanus!
MARTIUS	No more of this; it does offend my heart.
	Pray now, no more.
COMINIUS	Look, sir, your mother!
MARTIUS	O, 150
	You have, I know, petition'd all the gods
	For my prosperity. *Kneels.*
VOLUMNIA	Nay, my good soldier, up.
	My gentle Martius, worthy Caius, and
	By deed-achieving honor newly nam'd—
	What is it—Coriolanus—must I call thee? 155
	But O, thy wife!
MARTIUS	My gracious silence, hail!
	Wouldst thou have laugh'd had I come coffin'd home
	That weep'st to see me triumph? Ah, my dear,
	Such eyes the widows in Corioles wear
	And mothers that lack sons.
MENENIUS	Now the gods crown thee! 160
MARTIUS	And live you yet? [*To Valeria*] O my sweet lady, pardon.
VOLUMNIA	I know not where to turn. O, welcome home!
	And welcome, General! and y'are welcome all!
MENENIUS	A hundred thousand welcomes! I could weep
	And I could laugh; I am light and heavy. Welcome. 165
	A curse begin at very root on's heart
	That is not glad to see thee! You are three
	That Rome should dote on; yet, by the faith of men,

---

143. **alone Martius did fight**: Exaggeration. See 1.4.64 and 2.2.71-73. 149. **offend**: grieve. 156. **thy wife**: Clearly, Virgilia is an afterthought. See 1.3.1, above. 157-58. **laugh'd…weep'st**: A joke. Virgilia is crying with joy or relief. Martius jokes that she'd be happier were he dead. 160. **crown**: bless. 161. **live you yet**: The suggestion is that Coriolanus has been away some time, yet the battle seems to have been over before it even begins. See 1.3.69-95, above. 162. **I know not where to turn**: where to begin giving thanks for this safe return. These lines seem better suited to Virgilia than the strong-willed Volumnia. 165. **light and heavy**: light, thus delight, joyful, though heavy with emotion. 167. **not glad to see thee**: Pointed at the tribunes and, possibly, the people themselves. —**three**: Virgilia, Volumnia, Valeria; foreshadowing their entry at 5.3.21.sd. 168. **dote**: love.

We have some old crabtrees here at home that will not
Be grafted to your relish. Yet welcome, warriors!   170
We call a nettle but a nettle and
The faults of fools but folly.

COMINIUS   Ever right.

MARTIUS   Menenius, ever, ever.

HERALD   Give way there, and go on!

MARTIUS   [to *Volumnia and Virgilia*] Your hand, and yours!   175
Ere in our own house I do shade my head,
The good patricians must be visited,
From whom I have receiv'd not only greetings,
But with them charge of honors.

VOLUMNIA   I have liv'd
To see inherited my very wishes,   180
And the buildings of my fancy. Only
There's one thing wanting, which I doubt not but
Our Rome will cast upon thee.

MARTIUS   Know, good mother,
I had rather be their servant in my way
Than sway with them in theirs.

COMINIUS   On, to the Capitol!   185
        Flourish. Cornets. Exeunt in state, as before.

        Brutus and Sicinius [come forward].

BRUTUS   All tongues speak of him, and the bleared sights
Are spectacled to see him. Your prattling nurse
Into a rapture lets her baby cry
While she chats him. The kitchen malkin pins
Her richest lockram 'bout her reechy neck,   190
Clamb'ring the walls to eye him. Stalls, bulks, windows
Are smother'd up, leads fill'd, and ridges hors'd
With variable complexions, all agreeing
In earnestness to see him. Seld-shown flamens

169-170. **crabtrees...grafted**: Grafted trees bear sweeter fruit. Another insult directed to the tribunes, who are sour apples or sourpusses. 171. **nettle**: The tribunes, who are like thorns that sting, irritate. 179. **charge of honors**: He is cashiering his commission; the war is over. He pointedly does not mention the tribunes, who share power in Rome. 180. **inherited my very wishes**: Volumnia has lived through her son, who has been raised to fulfill her ambitions. See 3.2.108. 184-185. **servant...Than**: Martius knows that his mother has political ambitions for him, but he demurs. 186-187. **bleared sights/ Are spectacled**: Even those who need glasses are focused on him. 187-188. **prattling nurse...baby cry**: The normally attentive nurse ignores the child to see him. 189-191. **malkin...lockram...to eye him**: The reechy (greasy) maids put on their best dresses and clamor to see him. 191-194. **Stall, bulks, windows...to see him**: Every place is filled with people happy to see him.

Do press among the popular throngs and puff   195
To win a vulgar station. Our veil'd dames
Commit the war of white and damask in
Their nicely gauded cheeks to th' wanton spoil
Of Phœbus' burning kisses. Such a pother
As if that whatsoever god who leads him   200
Were slily crept into his human powers
And gave him graceful posture.

SICINIUS   On the sudden
I warrant him consul.

BRUTUS   Then our office may
During his power go sleep.

SICINIUS   He cannot temp'rately transport his honors   205
From where he should begin and end, but will
Lose those he hath won.

BRUTUS   In that there's comfort.

SICINIUS   Doubt not
The commoners, for whom we stand, but they
Upon their ancient malice will forget
With the least cause these his new honors; which   210
That he will give them make I as little question
As he is proud to do't.

BRUTUS   I heard him swear,
Were he to stand for consul, never would he
Appear i' th' market place, nor on him put
The napless vesture of humility,   215
Nor, showing (as the manner is) his wounds
To th' people, beg their stinking breaths.

196-199. **veil'd dames…burning kisses**: Modest maids wear makeup, their cheeks red, as if tanned by Phœbus, the sun. 199. **pother**: commotion. 200-201. **As if that whatsoever god who leads him/ Were slily crept into his human powers**: As if he were a god in human form. 202-203. **On the sudden/ I warrant him consul**: In other words, now that he is suddenly famous, I bet he'll run for consul. A consul was the highest elected office in Rome. According to tradition, only patricians/aristocrats could be consul, though in 367 BC plebeians won the right to stand for this position. Normally, two consuls were elected every year, but here only one consul is elected. If confirmed, Martius will, in effect, be dictator for a year. 204. **power go sleep**: If Martius is consul, they will be marginalized, ignored. 205. **He cannot temp'rately transport his honors**: Temperamentally, he's ill-suited to politics. 207. **there's comfort**: Comfort in the notion that he'll be ineffective. 209. **ancient malice will forget**: The plebeians will soon forget him. 213-214. **never would he/ Appear i' th' market place, nor on him put**: This proves true, though his pride/humility has nothing to do, per se, with his hatred of the people and his dislike of political office. 215. **The napless vesture of humility**: Shakespeare follows his Roman source here, North. See Kittredge's Introduction. 217. **stinking breath**: Even the tribunes hold the people in contempt.

SICINIUS   'Tis right.

BRUTUS   It was his word. O, he would miss it, rather
              Than carry it but by the suit of the gentry to him
              And the desire of the nobles.

SICINIUS   I wish no better   220
              Than have him hold that purpose and to put it
              In execution.

BRUTUS   'Tis most like he will.

SICINIUS   It shall be to him then, as our good wills,
              A sure destruction.

BRUTUS   So it must fall out
              To him or our authorities for an end.   225
              We must suggest the people in what hatred
              He still hath held them; that to's power he would
              Have made them mules, silenc'd their pleaders, and
              Dispropertied their freedoms; holding them,
              In human action and capacity,   230
              Of no more soul nor fitness for the world
              Than camels in the war, who have their provand
              Only for bearing burthens, and sore blows
              For sinking under them.

SICINIUS   This, as you say, suggested
              At some time when his soaring insolence   235
              Shall touch the people—which time shall not want
              If he be put upon't, and that's as easy
              As to set dogs on sheep—will be his fire
              To kindle their dry stubble; and their blaze
              Shall darken him forever.

                          Enter a Messenger.

BRUTUS   What's the matter?   240

MESSENGER   You are sent for to the Capitol. 'Tis thought
              That Martius shall be consul.
              I have seen the dumb men throng to see him and

---

219. **by the suit of the gentry**: Bypassing the traditional forms, which require the consent of the people.
220. **I wish no better**: In other words, that would be great, in that he would play into our hands. 224.
fall out: play out. 225. **To him or our authorities**: It's him or us. 226. **suggest**: insinuate. 227. **to's**
power: to give him this power. 229. **Dispropertied their freedoms**: Strip them of their rights. 232-33.
camels in the war, who have their provand/ Only for bearing burthens: Martius thinks of them as
pack animals, not as people. 235. **soaring**: rising, predatory, like an eagle or hawk. 237. **put upon't**:
given the opportunity. 238. **dogs on sheep**: Instinctive, Martius won't be able to stop himself. 240.
darken him forever: burn up, thus blacken, his reputation. 241. **thought**: heard or overheard, gossip.
243. **dumb**: silent, not a reference to intelligence.

The blind to hear him speak. Matrons flung gloves,
Ladies and maids their scarfs and handkerchers,   245
Upon him as he pass'd; the nobles bended
As to Jove's statue, and the commons made
A shower and thunder with their caps and shouts.
I never saw the like.

BRUTUS   Let's to the Capitol,
And carry with us ears and eyes for th' time,   250
But hearts for the event.

SICINIUS   Have with you.   *Exeunt.*

SCENE II. [*Rome. The Capitol.*]

Enter two Officers, to lay cushions, as it were in the Capitol.

1 OFFICER   Come, come, they are almost here.
How many stand for consulships?

2 OFFICER   Three, they say; but 'tis thought of every one Coriolanus will
carry it.

1 OFFICER   That's a brave fellow; but he's vengeance proud and loves not
the common people.   6

2 OFFICER   Faith, here hath been many great men that have flatter'd
the people, who ne'er loved them; and there be many that
they have loved, they know not wherefore; so that, if they
love they know not why, they hate upon no better a ground.
Therefore, for Coriolanus neither to care whether they love
or hate him manifests the true knowledge he has in their
disposition, and out of his noble carelessness lets them plainly
see't.   14

1 OFFICER   If he did not care whether he had their love or no, he waved
indifferently 'twixt doing them neither good nor harm; but
he seeks their hate with greater devotion than they can render

---

246. **bended**: bowed. 247. **Jove's statue**: As if he, Martius, were a god. See commentary at 1.1.243. 248.
A shower: Caps thrown in the air; it rained caps. 250-251. **ears and eyes…hearts**: Keep our wits about
us but hope that Martius falls; as outlined at 2.1.235-40, above.
SCENE 2
4. **carry it**: win the election. 5. **vengeance proud**: an oath, as in damn proud. 7. **flatter'd**: It is expected
that Martius will go through the motions and pretend that he loves the people. 9-10. **they love they
know not why**: The officers have little regard for the people's intellect. 13-14. **noble carelessness lets
them plainly see't**: Martius is too noble to flatter those he does not respect. 17. **he seeks their hate**:
Martius mocks the people.

it him and leaves nothing undone that may fully discover
him their opposite. Now to seem to affect the malice and
displeasure of the people is as bad as that which he dislikes—
to flatter them for their love.   21

2 OFFICER   He hath deserved worthily of his country; and his ascent is
not by such easy degrees as those who, having been supple
and courteous to the people, bonneted, without any further
deed to have them at all into their estimation and report; but
he hath so planted his honors in their eyes and his actions in
their hearts that for their tongues to be silent and not confess
so much were a kind of ingrateful injury; to report otherwise
were a malice that, giving itself the lie, would pluck reproof
and rebuke from every ear that heard it.   30

1 OFFICER   No more of him; he's a worthy man. Make way; they are
coming.

A sennet. Enter the Patricians and the Tribunes of the People,
Lictors before them; Martius, Menenius, Cominius the Consul.
Sicinius and Brutus take their places by themselves. Martius stands.

MENENIUS   Having determin'd of the Volsces and
To send for Titus Lartius, it remains,
As the main point of this our after-meeting,   35
To gratify his noble service that
Hath thus stood for his country. Therefore please you,
Most reverend and grave elders, to desire
The present consul and last general
In our well-found successes, to report   40
A little of that worthy work perform'd
By Caius Martius Coriolanus, whom
We met here both to thank, and to remember
With honors like himself.   [*Martius sits.*]

1 SENATOR   Speak, good Cominius.
Leave nothing out for length, and make us think   45
Rather our state's defective for requital

---

20. **as bad as that which he dislikes**: In other words, to mock the people is worse than to lie to them.
22-28. **deserved worthily...ingrateful injury**: Martius deserves the consulship more than others who
have already earned it, and the people, whether they like him or not, must recognize his worth or be
accused of ungratefulness. 31. **No more of him**: Let's not waste words. 33-37. **Having determin'd...
for his country**: Menenius enters in mid-sentence. He and the other senators are still working out
the details of the peace accord with the Volsces. Menenius' political dealings here contradict his
self-assessment at 2.1.40-56. 39. **present consul and last general**: Cominius. 44. **With honors like
himself**: As honorable as Martius himself. 46. **Rather our state's defective for requital**: The state owes
Martius more than it can ever repay.

Than we to stretch it out. [*To the Tribunes*] Masters o' th' people,
We do request your kindest ears, and after,
Your loving motion toward the common body
To yield what passes here.

SICINIUS   We are convented   50
Upon a pleasing treaty, and have hearts
Inclinable to honor and advance
The theme of our assembly.

BRUTUS   Which the rather
We shall be blest to do, if he remember
A kinder value of the people than   55
He hath hereto priz'd them at.

MENENIUS   That's off, that's off!
I would you rather had been silent. Please you
To hear Cominius speak?

BRUTUS   Most willingly;
But yet my caution was more pertinent
Than the rebuke you give it.

MENENIUS   He loves your people;   60
But tie him not to be their bedfellow.
Worthy Cominius, speak.
                                Martius rises, and offers to go away.
                                    Nay, keep your place.

1 SENATOR   Sit, Coriolanus. Never shame to hear
What you have nobly done.

MARTIUS   Your Honors' pardon.
I had rather have my wounds to heal again   65
Than hear say how I got them.

BRUTUS   Sir, I hope
My words disbench'd you not?

MARTIUS   No, sir. Yet oft,
When blows have made me stay, I fled from words.

---

47. **Masters o'th' people**: the tribunes. 50. **To yield**: agree to. 51. **pleasing treaty**: We must imagine that the Romans have settled with the Volsces in a manner that favored Rome. Contradicted at 1.10.2, above. 52. **Inclinable**: Agreeable. 53. **The theme**: The reason we are meeting. 54. **if he remember**: If Martius remembers to value the people. 59-60. **pertinent...rebuke**: Brutus argues that Menenius is being too sensitive; what he said was just and relevant to the vote. 60-61. **He loves your people;/ But tie him not to be their bedfellow**: Martius can love the common people of Rome without being one of them. 66-67. **I hope/ My words disbench'd you not**: I hope my words were not the reason why you almost walked out. Brutus infers that Martius is thin-skinned. 68. **I fled from words**: Martius admits his dislike of and unfitness for political life.

You sooth'd not, therefore hurt not; but your people,
I love them as they weigh—

MENENIUS   Pray now, sit down.   70

MARTIUS   I had rather have one scratch my head i' th' sun
When the alarum were struck than idly sit
To hear my nothings monster'd.   *Exit.*

MENENIUS   Masters of the people,
Your multiplying spawn how can he flatter
(That's thousand to one good one) when you now see   75
He had rather venture all his limbs for honor
Than one on's ears to hear it? Proceed, Cominius.

COMINIUS   I shall lack voice. The deeds of Coriolanus
Should not be utter'd feebly. It is held
That valor is the chiefest virtue and   80
Most dignifies the haver. If it be,
The man I speak of cannot in the world
Be singly counterpois'd. At sixteen years,
When Tarquin made a head for Rome, he fought
Beyond the mark of others. Our then-Dictator,   85
Whom with all praise I point at, saw him fight
When with his Amazonian chin he drove
The bristled lips before him. He bestrid
An o'erpress'd Roman and i' th' consul's view
Slew three opposers. Tarquin's self he met   90
And struck him on his knee. In that day's feats,
When he might act the woman in the scene,
He prov'd best man i' th' field and for his meed
Was brow-bound with the oak. His pupil age
Man-ent'red thus, he waxed like a sea,   95

---

70. **I love them as they weigh**: Menenius interrupts Martius, suggesting he was about to insult the people. 71-73. **I have rather...monster'd**: In essence, Martius would rather be seen as inactive during an emergency than sit and hear his deeds recited. This inability to accept thanks suggests a rooted inferiority complex, not its opposite. It may well be that Martius understands that the recital of his deeds will entail some exaggeration, which he deems unworthy. 74. **multiplying spawn**: Creatures that breed quickly. —**flatter**: The sense here is that one lie begets another. 78-79. **lack voice...feebly**: Run out of words, be unable to do Martius justice. 81. **haver**: The person who has it; behavior. 82-83. **cannot in the world/ Be singly counterpois'd**: Cannot be compared to any man living in the world today. 84. **Tarquin**: See 2.1.131, above. —**head**: attack. 85. **then-Dictator**: King Tarquin, also known as Aulus Posthumus Regillenius. 86. **point at**: recall. 87. **Amazonian chin**: Hairless, thus, womanlike. See 1.3.6. This may explain why Volumnia sent him to the wars so young. A girlish figure was a nearer surrogate for his mother than an adult, thus, manly, Martius. 88. **bestrid**: stood before. 91. **on his knee**: Cutting the knee would force Tarquin to kneel, thus yield. 92. **act the woman**: Fled like a woman in fear. 93. **meed**: honor, reward. 94. **brow-bound with the oak**: See 1.3.13. —**pupil age**: pupilage, apprenticeship. 95. **waxed like a sea**: rolled on; a natural, unstoppable force.

And in the brunt of seventeen battles since
He lurch'd all swords of the garland. For this last,
Before and in Corioles, let me say
I cannot speak him home. He stopp'd the fliers
And by his rare example made the coward   100
Turn terror into sport. As waves before
A vessel under sail, so men obey'd
And fell below his stem. His sword, death's stamp,
Where it did mark, it took. From face to foot
He was a thing of blood, whose every motion   105
Was tim'd with dying cries. Alone he ent'red
The mortal gate of th' city, which he painted
With shunless destiny; aidless came off,
And with a sudden reinforcement struck
Corioles like a planet. Now all's his,   110
When by-and-by the din of war gan pierce
His ready sense; then straight his doubled spirit
Requick'ned what in flesh was fatigate,
And to the battle came he, where he did
Run reeking o'er the lives of men, as if   115
'Twere a perpetual spoil; and till we call'd
Both field and city ours, he never stood
To ease his breast with panting.

MENENIUS   Worthy man!

1 SENATOR   He cannot but with measure fit the honors
Which we devise him.

COMINIUS   Our spoils he kick'd at   120
And look'd upon things precious as they were
The common muck of the world. He covets less
Than misery itself would give, rewards
His deeds with doing them, and is content
To spend the time to end it.

---

96. **in the brunt of seventeen battles since**: In the thick of seventeen subsequent battles. 97. **all swords of the garland**: bested all swords to win the ceremonial garland. 99. **I cannot speak him home**: I cannot do justice to his deeds. —**fliers**: deserters. 100-01. **coward/Turn terror**: Turned cowards into terrifying warriors. —**As waves**: Echoing the image of Martius and a natural force at 2.2.95, above. 104. **Where it did mark, it took**: Where he aimed, he killed. 105. **motion**: movement. 108. **shunless destiny**: Death, which no man escapes. —**aidless**: Without aid, alone. 110. **like a planet**: The seven traditional planets are Saturn, Jupiter, Mars, the Sun, Venus, Mercury and the moon. The image of them smashing into each other suggests complete chaos and nearly unthinkable destruction. 111. **gan peirce**: began again to pierce—i.e. he heard the clash of war. 113. **Requick'ned**: Reenergized. 115. **reeking**: Steaming with blood. 116. **perpetual spoil**: massacre. 117. **ours**: ours in victory. 119. **with measure**: Difficult. Perhaps "appropriate" or, following "multiplying," (2.2.74) without measure. 120-22. **spoils…common muck**: Martius was not interested in looting the city, just killing its citizens. In Roman terms, we are to see killing as far more virtuous than looting.

MENENIUS	He's right noble.	125
	Let him be call'd for.	
1 SENATOR	Call Coriolanus.	
OFFICER	He doth appear.	

Enter Martius.

MENENIUS The Senate, Coriolanus, are well pleas'd
To make thee consul.

MARTIUS   I do owe them still
My life and services.

MENENIUS   It then remains   130
That you do speak to the people.

MARTIUS   I do beseech you,
Let me o'erleap that custom; for I cannot
Put on the gown, stand naked, and entreat them
For my wounds' sake to give their suffrage. Please you
That I may pass this doing.

SICINIUS   Sir, the people   135
Must have their voices; neither will they bate
One jot of ceremony.

MENENIUS   Put them not to't.
Pray you go fit you to the custom and
Take to you, as your predecessors have,
Your honor with the form.

MARTIUS   It is a part   140
That I shall blush in acting, and might well
Be taken from the people.

BRUTUS [*to Sicinius*]   Mark you that?

MARTIUS To brag unto them, "Thus I did, and thus!"
Show them th' unaching scars which I should hide,
As if I had receiv'd them for the hire   145
Of their breath only!

---

125. **right noble**: highly honorable. 131. **beseech you**: beg you. 132. **o'erleap**: skip over, avoid. 134. **to give their suffrage**: to gain their vote, endorsement. 136. **bate**: abate, lose, give up. 138. **predecessors**: Martius is simply being asked to go through a ritual all Roman consuls have done before him. Since it is a Roman and aristocratic form or custom, his inability to do so suggests that he (a) feels unworthy; and/ or (b) his subsequent behavior shows not only a contempt for the plebeians but also for the patricians— see 2.2.120-23, below. 141. **blush**: makeup applied by women and actors; suggests that his falseness will cause him embarrassment. 142. **taken from the people**: Martius seems unconcerned that he is already encroaching on the people's rights. 144. **unaching**: No longer hurting, thus without merit; the words of a masochist. 145. **reciev'd them for the hire**: Martius did not fight for the loot or for the political power; yet, if so, why is he standing for consul?

MENENIUS	Do not stand upon't.
	We recommend to you, Tribunes of the People,
	Our purpose to them; and to our noble consul
	Wish we all joy and honor.
1 SENATOR	To Coriolanus come all joy and honor! 150

Flourish. Cornets. Then exeunt. Manent Sicinius and Brutus.

BRUTUS	You see how he intends to use the people.
SICINIUS	May they perceive's intent! He will require them
	As if he did contemn what he requested
	Should be in them to give.
BRUTUS	Come, we'll inform them
	Of our proceedings here. On th' market place 155
	I know they do attend us. [*Exeunt.*]

SCENE III. [*Rome. The Forum.*]

Enter seven or eight Citizens.

1 CITIZEN	Once if he do require our voices, we ought not to deny him.
2 CITIZEN	We may, sir, if we will.
3 CITIZEN	We have power in ourselves to do it, but it is a power that we have no power to do; for if he show us his wounds and tell us his deeds, we are to put our tongues into those wounds and speak for them. So, if he tell us his noble deeds, we must also tell him our noble acceptance of them. Ingratitude is monstrous; and for the multitude to be ingrateful were to make a monster of the multitude, of the which we being members, should bring ourselves to be monstrous members.
1 CITIZEN	And to make us no better thought of, a little help will serve;

---

146. **Do not stand upon't**: Enigmatic. If addressed to the tribunes, it might be a directive: "We don't need to do this"—see 2.2.134; if directed to Martius, it might be "Don't be silly; just do it and be done with it." 148. **to our noble consul**: Menenius suggests that Martius is already consul; that it is a done deal. 152. **contemn what he requested**: Whatever is hateful to Martius is unnecessary; thus, the tribunes suggest that Martius, hating the people, will ignore or reject their demands.
SCENE III
1. **require our voices**: ask for our endorsement. 3-4. **it is a power that we have no power to do**: This is a ritual. If Martius plays along, so will the people. 7-8. **Ingratitude is monstrous**: The idea here is of social obligation. Yet Martius, in denying the people food, has shown a contempt for that concept.

for once we stood up about the corn, he himself stuck not to
call us the many-headed multitude.   13

3 CITIZEN   We have been call'd so of many; not that our heads are some
brown, some black, some abram, some bald, but that our wits
are so diversely color'd. And truly I think, if all our wits were
to issue out of one skull, they would fly east, west, north,
south, and their consent of one direct way should be at once
to all the points o' th' compass.

2 CITIZEN   Think you so? Which way do you judge my wit would fly?

3 CITIZEN   Nay, your wit will not so soon out as another man's will. 'Tis
strongly wedg'd up in a blockhead. But if it were at liberty,
'twould sure southward.   23

2 CITIZEN   Why that way?

3 CITIZEN   To lose itself in a fog; where being three parts melted away
with rotten dews, the fourth would return for conscience
sake, to help to get thee a wife.

2 CITIZEN   You are never without your tricks. You may, you may!

3 CITIZEN   Are you all resolv'd to give your voices? But that's no matter,
the greater part carries it. I say, if he would incline to the
people, there was never a worthier man.   31

Enter Martius in a gown of humility, with Menenius.

Here he comes, and in the gown of humility. Mark his
behavior. We are not to stay all together, but to come by him
where he stands, by ones, by twos, and by threes. He's to
make his requests by particulars; wherein every one of us has
a single honor, in giving him our own voices with our own
tongues. Therefore follow me, and I'll direct you how you
shall go by him.   38

ALL   Content, content!   [*Exeunt Citizens.*]

12-13. **stuck not to call us the many-headed multitude**: Martius insulting them; compared to the
monstrous hydra, a snake with nine heads, killed by Hercules. The comparison is apt in that Hercules,
also a great warrior, died when he wore a poisoned or acid-drenched vest. Martius, about to wear
the vestment of humility (2.3.31.sd), will find the process nearly as painful. 15. **abram**: blond. 16.
diversely color'd: Of differing complexions. The people are of many heads and many minds. 19. **points
o'th' compass**: Their brains would fly in all directions. Even the people admit that they are clueless
and giddy. This may be a case of Shakespeare's personal opinion popping through the mouths of his
characters. 22. **blockhead**: This man's wits can't fly out of his head, since his head is so thick. Pun,
insult. 23. **southward**: damp, therefore infectious and deadly. 27. **get thee a wife**: Apparently only a
fool wants one. 28. **tricks**: jokes. —**You may**: You may have your joke. 30. **the greater part carries**:
Unanimous consent is not required. This is a popular vote. 35. **particulars**: His particular reasons for
being consul; his social platform. 39. **Content**: Agreed.

MENENIUS	O sir, you are not right. Have you not known 40 The worthiest men have done't?
MARTIUS	What must I say? "I pray, sir"—Plague upon't! I cannot bring My tongue to such a pace. "Look, sir, my wounds. I got them in my country's service, when Some certain of your brethren roar'd, and ran 45 From th' noise of our own drums."
MENENIUS	O me, the gods! You must not speak of that. You must desire them To think upon you.
MARTIUS	Think upon me? Hang 'em! I would they would forget me, like the virtues Which our divines lose by 'em.
MENENIUS	You'll mar all. 50 I'll leave you. Pray you speak to 'em. I pray you, In wholesome manner. *Exit.*

Enter three of the Citizens.

MARTIUS	Bid them wash their faces And keep their teeth clean. So, here comes a brace. You know the cause, sir, of my standing here.
3 CITIZEN	We do, sir. Tell us what hath brought you to't. 55
MARTIUS	Mine own desert.
2 CITIZEN	Your own desert?
MARTIUS	Ay, not mine own desire.
3 CITIZEN	How? Not your own desire?
MARTIUS	No, sir, 'twas never my desire yet to trouble the poor with begging. 61
3 CITIZEN	You must think, if we give you anything, we hope to gain by you.

---

40. **not right**: Not comfortable. 41. **worthiest men have done't**: See 2.2.138, option (b). 42-43. **Plague upon't**: An oath. —**I cannot bring/My tongue to such a pace**: Pace as in horse trot. In other words, I can't trot out the words, suggesting Martius feels that lying is akin to being tamed, broken, or defeated. 45. **roar'd**: Presumably in fear. 48. **think upon you**: Think well of you. 50. **divines lose by 'em**: The priestly or devout waste their time on them. 50. **mar**: ruin. 52. **wholesome**: kindly. 53. **brace**: a pair of fowl; as in a brace of grouse; also, foul, playing upon their bad breath in 2.3.53. 55. **Tell us what hath brought you to't**: Tell us your recent biography. 56. **desert**: deserving. 58. **desire**: No, it seems to have been his mother's. See 2.1.105 and 3.2.108. 60-61. **trouble the poor with begging**: Ironic, and while not quite an insult, is not as warm-hearted as the ritual demands.

MARTIUS	Well then, I pray, your price o' th' consulship?	
1 CITIZEN	The price is, to ask it kindly.	65
MARTIUS	Kindly, sir, I pray let me ha't. I have wounds to show you, which shall be yours in private. Your good voice, sir. What say you?	
2 CITIZEN	You shall ha't, worthy sir.	
MARTIUS	A match, sir. There's in all two worthy voices begg'd. I have your alms. Adieu.	71
3 CITIZEN	But this is something odd.	
2 CITIZEN	An 'twere to give again—but 'tis no matter.	

Exeunt [the three Citizens]

Enter two other Citizens.

MARTIUS	Pray you now, if it may stand with the tune of your voices that I may be consul, I have here the customary gown.	75
1 CITIZEN	You have deserved nobly of your country, and you have not deserved nobly.	
MARTIUS	Your enigma?	
1 CITIZEN	You have been a scourge to her enemies; you have been a rod to her friends. You have not indeed loved the common people.	81
MARTIUS	You should account me the more virtuous that I have not been common in my love. I will, sir, flatter my sworn brother, the people, to earn a dearer estimation of them. 'Tis a condition they account gentle; and since the wisdom of their choice is rather to have my hat than my heart, I will practise the insinuating nod and be off to them most counterfeitly: that is, sir, I will counterfeit the bewitchment of some popular man and give it bountiful to the desirers. Therefore, beseech you I may be consul.	90

---

64. **price**: Martius disdains loot or any mercenary ambition, so this is clearly meant as a insult. 65. **to ask it kindly**: The reply is one of the few times the poor of Rome come off well; their request is merely that Martius behave himself. 67. **yours in private**: Scornful. A veiled threat? Give me your vote, or I'll beat you in private. 69. **You shall ha't**: You shall have it; not picking up on Martius' scorn in the previous line. 71. **alms**: charity, playing on 2.3.60-61, above. 73. **An 'twere to give again**: If I could vote again, I'd do it differently. Interestingly, these people seem bound by their private declaration to Martius, suggesting that the ritual functions as a personal bond between the consul and the people of Rome. 80. **rod to her friends**: Just as cruel to the poor of Rome. 82-90. **You should account me...I may be consul**: A difficult and deliberately convoluted speech. Martius now realizes that he can insult the people by baffling them with wordplay. The gist of the speech is: "I have always disliked you, but have done it honestly. If you prefer to be lied to, I'll lie to you. Now give me the consulship, pretty please."

2 CITIZEN	We hope to find you our friend; and therefore give you our voices heartily.
1 CITIZEN	You have received many wounds for your country.
MARTIUS	I will not seal your knowledge with showing them. I will make much of your voices, and so trouble you no farther. 95
BOTH	The gods give you joy, sir, heartily! *[Exeunt Citizens.]*
MARTIUS	Most sweet voices!

Better it is to die, better to starve,
Than crave the hire which first we do deserve.
Why in this wolvish toge should I stand here   100
To beg of Hob and Dick that do appear
Their needless vouches? Custom calls me to't.
What custom wills, in all things should we do't,
The dust on antique time would lie unswept,
And mountainous error be too highly heapt   105
For truth to o'erpeer. Rather than fool it so,
Let the high office and the honor go
To one that would do thus. I am half through;
The one part suffer'd, the other will I do.

Enter three Citizens more.

Here come moe voices.—   110
Your voices! For your voices I have fought;
Watch'd for your voices; for your voices bear
Of wounds two dozen odd; battles thrice six
I have seen and heard of; for your voices have
Done many things, some less, some more. Your voices!   115
Indeed I would be consul.

1 CITIZEN	He has done nobly and cannot go without any honest man's voice.
2 CITIZEN	Therefore let him be consul. The gods give him joy and make him good friend to the people! 120
ALL	Amen, amen. God save thee, noble Consul!
MARTIUS	Worthy voices! *[Exeunt Citizens.]*

92. **heartily**: We mean that sincerely. 97. **sweet voices**: Ironic, said with contempt. 99. **hire which first we do deserve**: To ask for that which is owed. 100. **wolvish toge**: Traditional Roman garb; Romulus and Remus, the founders of Rome, were said to be raised by wolves. 101. **Hob and Dick**: Joe Six-Pack, the average guy. 102. **needless**: Martius sees the ritual as a waste of time. 103-106. **Custom....For truth to o'erpeer**: Custom obscures reality. The people do not deserve the respect the ritual entails. 106. **fool it**: lie foolishly. 108. **do thus**: deserves it. 110. **moe**: more. 113. **two dozen…thrice six**: 24 and 18; Martius assumes the people can't count. He again insists that he is paying for what is rightfully his, despite the exchange at 2.3.65-68, above. 117-18. **cannot go without any honest man's voice**: He has done what was requested.

Enter Menenius, with Brutus and Sicinius.

MENENIUS   You have stood your limitation, and the tribunes
Endue you with the people's voice. Remains
That, in th' official marks invested, you   125
Anon do meet the Senate.

MARTIUS   Is this done?

SICINIUS   The custom of request you have discharg'd.
The people do admit you, and are summon'd
To meet anon upon your approbation.

MARTIUS   Where? at the Senate House?

SICINIUS   There, Coriolanus.   130

MARTIUS   May I change these garments?

SICINIUS   You may, sir.

MARTIUS   That I'll straight do and, knowing myself again,
Repair to th' Senate House.

MENENIUS   I'll keep you company.—Will you along?

BRUTUS   We stay here for the people.

SICINIUS   Fare you well.   135

Exeunt Martius and Menenius.
He has it now; and by his looks, methinks,
'Tis warm at's heart.

BRUTUS   With a proud heart he wore
His humble weeds. Will you dismiss the people?

Enter the Plebeians.

SICINIUS   How now, my masters? Have you chose this man?

1 CITIZEN   He has our voices, sir.   140

BRUTUS   We pray the gods he may deserve your loves.

2 CITIZEN   Amen, sir. To my poor unworthy notice,
He mock'd us when he begg'd our voices.

3 CITIZEN   Certainly, he flouted us downright.

---

123. **limitation**: The least amount of time required for the ritual. 124. **Endue you**: Sanctify you. 124-126. **Remains/That, in th' official marks invested, you/Anon do meet the Senate**: All that remains, according to protocol, is that you now meet with the Senate. 129. **upon your approbation**: With your approval. The tone is perfunctory. 131. **May I**: Given that he is addressing the tribune Sicinius Velutus, we must imagine that the tone here is scornful. 132. **knowing myself again**: Dressed as himself; and presumably, no longer mouthing the words of a beggar. 136. **it**: the consulship. 137. **warm at's heart**: Happy to have it, though possibly Sicinius Velutus means "heartburn"—i.e. that he's sick from having undergone the ritual of asking the people for something. 141. **loves**: faith. 144. **flouted**: mocked.

| 1 CITIZEN | No, 'tis his kind of speech; he did not mock us. | 145 |

2 CITIZEN	Not one amongst us, save yourself, but says
	He us'd us scornfully. He should have show'd us
	His marks of merit, wounds receiv'd for's country.

| SICINIUS | Why, so he did, I am sure. |

| ALL | No, no! No man saw 'em. |

3 CITIZEN	He said he had wounds which he could show in private,	150
	And with his hat, thus waving it in scorn,
	"I would be consul," says he. "Aged custom
	But by your voices will not so permit me.
	Your voices therefore!" When we granted that,
	Here was "I thank you for your voices, thank you!	155
	Your most sweet voices! Now you have left your voices,
	I have no further with you." Was not this mockery?

SICINIUS	Why either were you ignorant to see't,
	Or, seeing it, of such childish friendliness
	To yield your voices?

BRUTUS	Could you not have told him	160
	As you were lesson'd? When he had no power
	But was a petty servant to the state,
	He was your enemy; ever spake against
	Your liberties and the charters that you bear
	I' th' body of the weal; and now, arriving	165
	A place of potency and sway o' th' state,
	If he should still malignantly remain
	Fast foe to th' plebeii, your voices might

---

146. **save**: except. 148. **marks of merit**: Out of respect, he should have shown the people his wounds. 152. **Aged**: Old, therefore outmoded, quaint. 157. **have no further with you**: have no further dealings with you. 159. **childish**: naïve, unsophisticated. 161. **As you were lesson'd**: as we previously discussed and planned. 162. **petty**: unimportant. 163. **spake**: spoke. 165. **weal**: commonweal, the republic of Rome. 166. **potency and sway**: the powerful post of consul. 167-69. **If he should...curses to yourselves**: If Martius continues to hate you, his new post will mean hard times for you, so you voted for the wrong guy.

Be curses to yourselves. You should have said
That, as his worthy deeds did claim no less   170
Than what he stood for, so his gracious nature
Would think upon you for your voices and
Translate his malice towards you into love,
Standing your friendly lord.

SICINIUS   Thus to have said,
As you were fore-advis'd, had touch'd his spirit   175
And tried his inclination; from him pluck'd
Either his gracious promise, which you might,
As cause had call'd you up, have held him to;
Or else it would have gall'd his surly nature,
Which easily endures not article   180
Tying him to aught. So, putting him to rage,
You should have ta'en th' advantage of his choler
And pass'd him unelected.

BRUTUS   Did you perceive
He did solicit you in free contempt
When he did need your loves, and do you think   185
That his contempt shall not be bruising to you
When he hath power to crush? Why, had your bodies
No heart among you? Or had you tongues to cry
Against the rectorship of judgment?

SICINIUS   Have you,
Ere now, denied the asker, and now again,   190
Of him that did not ask but mock, bestow
Your su'd-for tongues?

3 CITIZEN   He's not confirm'd; we may deny him yet.

2 CITIZEN   And will deny him.
I'll have five hundred voices of that sound.   195

1 CITIZEN   I twice five hundred, and their friends to piece 'em.

169-83. **You should have said……his surly nature...pass'd him unelected**: You should have told Martius that his courage deserved reward, and then seen if he reacted with love or contempt. In short, Martius would have revealed his true self. If Martius had acted kindly, then you could have elected him; if fiercely, then rejected him. This is in fact the way the discussion turned at 2.3.62-65. Brutus' and Sicinius' responses show frustration and contempt for the people, who, after all, acted out of good will. 184. **free**: open, undisguised. 186. **bruising to you**: Hard on you. 187. **heart**: Brains might be a better word, as the people did act, if somewhat formulaically, with an open and generous spirit. See 2.3.65, above. 190. **denied the asker**: Suggests that the people have turned down other candidates, though not one as deserving as Martius. Deserve here is defined by battle scars. See the text of 2.3.123-24, above. 193. **He's not confirm'd**: True in that he has yet to be confirmed by the Senate, but their vote has been cast, counted, and ratified. See 2.3.128-29, above, and Martius' prophetic comments at 1.1.150-64, above. 195. **that sound**: that agree. 196. **piece 'em**: match them.

BRUTUS	Get you hence instantly, and tell those friends
	They have chose a consul that will from them take
	Their liberties; make them of no more voice
	Than dogs, that are as often beat for barking 200
	As therefore kept to do so.
SICINIUS	Let them assemble;
	And, on a safer judgment, all revoke
	Your ignorant election. Enforce his pride
	And his old hate unto you. Besides, forget not
	With what contempt he wore the humble weed; 205
	How in his suit he scorn'd you; but your loves,
	Thinking upon his services, took from you
	The apprehension of his present portance,
	Which most gibingly, ungravely, he did fashion
	After the inveterate hate he bears you.
BRUTUS	Lay 210
	A fault on us, your tribunes, that we labor'd,
	No impediment between, but that you must
	Cast your election on him.
SICINIUS	Say you chose him
	More after our commandment than as guided
	By your own true affections; and that your minds, 215
	Preoccupied with what you rather must do
	Than what you should, made you against the grain
	To voice him consul. Lay the fault on us.
BRUTUS	Ay, spare us not. Say we read lectures to you,
	How youngly he began to serve his country, 220
	How long continued; and what stock he springs of,
	The noble house o' th' Marcians; from whence came
	That Ancus Martius, Numa's daughter's son,
	Who after great Hostilius here was King;
	Of the same house Publius and Quintus were, 225

199-200. **make them of no more voice/Than dogs...for barking**: Under Martius, the people will be beaten like dogs for expressing their will. 201. **kept to do so**: Stay resolved. Suggesting the unreliability of the people and, thus, ironically confirming Martius' opinion at 1.1.50-64, above. 203. **ignorant**: hasty. —**Enforce**: Awaken, entice. 205. **humble weed**: the gown of humility; see 2.3.31 sd. and 2.3.131. 206. **his suit**: his asking. 208. **portance**: import, meaning. 209. **gibingly, ungravely**: mockingly, with contempt. 210-14. **inveterate**: incurable. —**Lay/A fault on us...Say you chose him/More after our commandment**: If you feel embarrassed by withdrawing your support, blame it on us. There is a bit of politics going on here. If the people say the tribunes were for Martius, then Brutus and Sicinius are not to blame for the collapse of Martius' public support. 216. **must do**: called for by ritual. 218. **voice him**: elect him. 223. **Ancus Marcius**: Some background on Martius' family. The second king of Rome (715-673 BCE).

That our best water brought by conduits hither;
And [Censorinus, who was] nobly nam'd so,
Twice being [by the people chosen] Censor,
Was his great ancestor.

SICINIUS   One thus descended,
That hath beside well in his person wrought   230
To be set high in place, we did commend
To your remembrances; but you have found,
Scaling his present bearing with his past,
That he's your fixed enemy, and revoke
Your sudden approbation.

BRUTUS   Say you ne'er had done't   235
(Harp on that still) but by our putting on;
And presently, when you have drawn your number,
Repair to th' Capitol.

ALL   We will so. Almost all
Repent in their election.
              Exeunt Plebeians.

BRUTUS   Let them go on.
This mutiny were better put in hazard   240
Than stay, past doubt, for greater.
If, as his nature is, he fall in rage
With their refusal, both observe and answer
The vantage of his anger.

SICINIUS   To th' Capitol, come.
We will be there before the stream o' th' people;   245
And this shall seem, as partly 'tis, their own,
Which we have goaded onward.   *Exeunt.*

231-34. **commend/ To your remembrances**: We reminded you. —**but you have found…That he's your fixed enemy**: Despite Martius' deeds and family connections, the fact that he hates the people so is reason enough for the people to withdraw their nomination. 235. **ne'er had done't**: voted for Martius. 236. **but by our putting on**: except for our pressuring you to do so. 237. **drawn your number**: When the 1,500 supporters are assembled. See 2.3.196, above. 238. **Repair**: Make your way. 240. **in hazard**: in play, at risk. 241. **for greater**: Risked to avoid greater hazards, i.e. the election of Martius. 244. **vantage**: visage and condition. 246. **their own**: Echoing 2.3.213-18, above. The tribunes will continue to argue that they had nothing to do with this sudden insurrection.

Act III

Scene I. [*Rome. A street.*]

Cornets. Enter Martius, Menenius, all the Gentry, Cominius,
Titus Lartius, and other Senators.

MARTIUS   Tullus Aufidius, then, had made new head?

LARTIUS   He had, my lord, and that it was which caus'd
Our swifter composition.

MARTIUS   So then the Volsces stand but as at first,
Ready, when time shall prompt them, to make road   5
Upon's again.

COMINIUS   They are worn, Lord Consul, so
That we shall hardly in our ages see
Their banners wave again.

MARTIUS   Saw you Aufidius?

LARTIUS   On safeguard he came to me, and did curse
Against the Volsces for they had so vilely   10
Yielded the town. He is retir'd to Antium.

MARTIUS   Spoke he of me?

LARTIUS   He did, my lord.

MARTIUS   How? what?

LARTIUS   How often he had met you sword to sword;
That of all things upon the earth he hated
Your person most; that he would pawn his fortunes   15
To hopeless restitution, so he might
Be call'd your vanquisher.

MARTIUS   At Antium lives he?

LARTIUS   At Antium.

Act III. Scene I.
1. **new head**: A new attack upon Roman territory. 3. **swifter composition**: swift meeting or reaction. 4. **but as at first**: as strong as ever. 5. **road**: inroad. 6. **Upon's**: Upon us. —**worn**: Perhaps, frayed, weakened by prior battle, ready for their final destruction. —**Lord Consul**: Cominius has apparently resigned as Consul in favor of the newly-appointed Martius, who now leads the war council. 9. **safeguard**: safe-conduct. 11. **town**: of Corioli, as seen throughout 1.4, above. —**Antium**: Or Anzio is about 57 km south of Rome. 15-16. **pawn his fortunes/ To hopeless restitution**: trade all he owns, including, presumably, his life. In other words, deal with the devil.

MARTIUS	I wish I had a cause to seek him there,
	To oppose his hatred fully. Welcome home. 20

Enter Sicinius and Brutus.

	Behold, these are the tribunes† of the people,
	The tongues o' th' common mouth. I do despise them,
	For they do prank them in authority
	Against all noble sufferance.
SICINIUS	Pass no further.
MARTIUS	Ha! What is that? 25
BRUTUS	It will be dangerous to go on. No further.
MARTIUS	What makes this change?
MENENIUS	The matter?
COMINIUS	Hath he not pass'd the noble and the common?
BRUTUS	Cominius, no.‡
MARTIUS	Have I had children's voices? 30
1 SENATOR	Tribunes, give way. He shall to th' market place.
BRUTUS	The people are incens'd against him.
SICINIUS	Stop,
	Or all will fall in broil.
MARTIUS	Are these your herd?
	Must these have voices, that can yield them now
	And straight disclaim their tongues? What are your offices?
	You being their mouths, why rule you not their teeth?
	Have you not set them on?
MENENIUS	Be calm, be calm.

---

19. **I wish I had a cause to seek him there**: Are we to suppose that Aufidius is not involved in the new attack upon Rome? 23. **prank them**: Deceitfully and disloyally lead the people. 24. **sufferance**: beyond patience. 26. **dangerous to go on**: Considering that Martius has single-handedly faced down an army, this seems unlikely. 30. **children's voices**: Unthinking, easily swayed, unreliable. 33-37. **broil**: violence. The people will attack Martius and his supporters, the Senate. —**herd...Have you not set them on**: Martius considers the people to be a pack, guided by the predatory tribunes.

---

† The tribunes: In the recent Olde Globe production (2009; dir. Darko Tresnjak), the tribunes (James Newcomb and Grant Goodman), "an eye-catching Mutt-and-Jeff pair," are dressed in newsboy caps; later, after Martius' exile, they sport more expensive suits, a sign of their growing affluence (Pam Kragen, *North County Times*, July 15, 2009).

‡ Condemning Martius, now called Coriolanus: In the BBC TV version (1984; dir. Elijah Moshinsky), this is no court of law but an upstart mob. Coriolanus (Alan Howard) seems rather to be enjoying himself, as if he did not think the people really had this mettle.

MARTIUS	It is a purpos'd thing and grows by plot
	To curb the will of the nobility.
	Suffer't, and live with such as cannot rule 40
	Nor ever will be rul'd.
BRUTUS	Call't not a plot.
	The people cry you mock'd them; and of late,
	When corn was given them gratis, you repin'd;
	Scandal'd the suppliants for the people, call'd them
	Time-pleasers, flatterers, foes to nobleness. 45
MARTIUS	Why, this was known before.
BRUTUS	Not to them all.
MARTIUS	Have you inform'd them sithence?
BRUTUS	How? I inform them?
MARTIUS	You are like to do such business.
BRUTUS	Not unlike
	Each way to better yours.
MARTIUS	Why then should I be consul? By yond clouds, 50
	Let me deserve so ill as you, and make me
	Your fellow tribune.
SICINUS	You show too much of that
	For which the people stir. If you will pass
	To where you are bound, you must enquire your way,
	Which you are out of, with a gentler spirit, 55
	Or never be so noble as a consul
	Nor yoke with him for tribune.
MENENIUS	Let's be calm.
COMINIUS	The people are abus'd, set on. This palt'ring
	Becomes not Rome; nor has Coriolanus
	Deserv'd this so dishonour'd rub, laid falsely 60
	I' th' plain way of his merit.

---

38. **purpos'd**: planned. 40. **cannot rule**: In reference to the poor. 43. **corn was given them gratis**: free corn to the poor. —**repin'd**: objected. 47. **sithence**: since then. —**How? I inform them**: Who, me? 48. **like**: likely. 48-49. **Not unlike/ Each way to better yours**: Difficult. Perhaps, if we turn the people against you, we merely imitate you. 50-52. **consul…make me/ Your fellow tribune**: Ironic. Martius suggest that he should be a tribune, since that post has more power than consul. 52. **of that**: Pride? Arrogance? Scorn? 54-55. **enquire your way,/ Which you are out of**: Out of your depth, in need of our help. 58. **set on**: misled. —**palt'ring**: petty politicking. 60. **dishonour'd rub**: base insult, abuse. —**laid falsely**: planned treacherously.

MARTIUS	Tell me of corn!
	This was my speech, and I will speak't again—
MENENIUS	Not now! not now!
1 SENATOR	Not in this heat, sir, now.
MARTIUS	Now, as I live, I will! My nobler friends,
	I crave their pardons. 65
	For the mutable, rank-scented meiny, let them
	Regard me as I do not flatter, and
	Therein behold themselves. I say again,
	In soothing them we nourish 'gainst our Senate
	The cockle of rebellion, insolence, sedition, 70
	Which we ourselves have plough'd for, sow'd, and scatter'd
	By mingling them with us, the honor'd number,
	Who lack not virtue, no, nor power, but that
	Which they have given to beggars.
MENENIUS	Well, no more.
1 SENATOR	No more words, we beseech you.
MARTIUS	How? No more? 75
	As for my country I have shed my blood,
	Not fearing outward force, so shall my lungs
	Coin words till their decay against those measles
	Which we disdain should tetter us, yet sought
	The very way to catch them.
BRUTUS	You speak o' th' people 80
	As if you were a god to punish, not
	A man of their infirmity.
SICINUS	'Twere well
	We let the people know't.
MENENIUS	What, what? his choler?

---

62. **This was my speech**: Alluding to a speech he made, presumably to the Senate, in which he argued that Rome should not give corn to the poor. 65. **pardons**: for disagreeing with the Senators in favor of feeding the poor. 66. **mutable, rank-scented meiny**: unreliable, stinking impoverished of Rome. 67-68. **Regard me...behold themselves**: Martius, ever-constant, does not change. He is like a mirror; the people, mutable images which pass. Related to the idea of fame/immortality, which Martius has won in battle. Men and women are merely transient shadows; Martius' exploits are the stuff of record, thus, a permanent and fixed object. 69. **nourish**: By feeding the poor, by giving into their demands, we are feeding insurrection. 70. **cockle**: seed. 72. **By mingling them with us**: Martius means the appointment of the tribunes, representatives of the people. See 1.1.198. 74. **beggars**: The people and their tribunes. 77-79. **fearing outward force, so shall my lungs/...against those measles/...tetter us**: Roughly, I'm not afraid of the enemy, so why shouldn't I speak out against this disease undermining Rome's strength? See commentary at 1.3.98. 82. **infirmity**: Mortal, with weakness. 83. **choler**: anger.

MARTIUS	Choler? Were I as patient as the midnight sleep,
	By Jove, 'twould be my mind!

SICINUS   It is a mind   85
That shall remain a poison where it is,
Not poison any further.

MARTIUS   Shall remain?
Hear you this Triton of the minnows? Mark you
His absolute "shall"?

COMINIUS   'Twas from the canon.

MARTIUS   "Shall"?
O good but most unwise patricians! Why,   90
You grave but reckless senators, have you thus
Given Hydra here to choose an officer
That with his peremptory "shall," being but
The horn and noise o' th' monster's, wants not spirit
To say he'll turn your current in a ditch   95
And make your channel his? If he have power,
Then vail your ignorance; if none, awake
Your dangerous lenity. If you are learn'd,
Be not as common fools; if you are not,
Let them have cushions by you. You are plebeians   100
If they be senators; and they are no less
When, both your voices blended, the great'st taste
Most palates theirs. They choose their magistrate;
And such a one as he, who puts his "shall,"
His popular "shall," against a graver bench   105
Than ever frown'd in Greece. By Jove himself,
It makes the consuls base! and my soul aches

---

84. **midnight sleep**: still, as one in deep sleep. 86. **where it is**: without further power. 88. **Triton of the minnows**: Ironic. A king of little fish. Paltry, insignificant.—**Mark you**: Ironic, mocking. Do you hear this guy? 89. **canon**: A canonical book, like the Bible, spoken with authority. Cominius obviously agrees with Martius that the tribunes have, in effect, seized power. 90. **unwise patricians**: Martius reminds them that he warned them of this. See 3.1.64-74, above. 92. **Hydra**: See 2.3.9, above. 93. **peremptory**: authoritative. 94. **horn and noise...wants not spirit**: The people express their will, but it's all noise and bluster. They have no real power—no army to back up their demands. 95-98. **your current in a ditch/ And make your channel his**: Usurp and despoil. In other words, redirect your wide river into a narrow ditch (polluted cesspool?) and call the water your own. —**If he have power,/... lenity**: Roughly, If he has power, curb it; if he is powerless, then stop trying to empower him. 100. **cushions**: For fools. 102. **great'st taste**: There are more poor than rich, ergo, if the plebeians can now become senators, the poor will have a greater voice, therefore more tongues, therefore more taste. 103. **palates**: mouths. 105. **graver bench**: wiser senator. 106. **Than ever frowned in Greece**: A reference, perhaps, to the Stoics, philosophers who saw life as a cup essentially half full. —**Jove**: King of the Roman Gods, who, ironically, claimed that title by insurrection/usurpation. 107. **base**: dishonorable.

To know, when two authorities are up,
Neither supreme, how soon confusion
May enter 'twixt the gap of both and take   110
The one by th' other.

COMINIUS   Well, on to th' market place.

MARTIUS   Whoever gave that counsel to give forth
The corn o' th' storehouse gratis, as 'twas us'd
Sometime in Greece—

MENENIUS   Well, well, no more of that.

MARTIUS   Though there the people had more absolute pow'r—   115
I say they nourish'd disobedience, fed
The ruin of the state.

BRUTUS   Why, shall the people give
One that speaks thus their voice?

MARTIUS   I'll give my reasons,
More worthier than their voices. They know the corn
Was not our recompense, resting well assur'd   120
They ne'er did service for't. Being press'd to th' war
Even when the navel of the state was touch'd,
They would not thread the gates. This kind of service
Did not deserve corn gratis. Being i' th' war,
Their mutinies and revolts, wherein they show'd   125
Most valor, spoke not for them. Th' accusation
Which they have often made against the Senate,
All cause unborn, could never be the motive
Of our so frank donation. Well, what then?
How shall this beesom multitude digest   130
The Senate's courtesy? Let deeds express
What's like to be their words: "We did request it;
We are the greater poll, and in true fear
They gave us our demands." Thus we debase

---

111. **one by th'other**: When both authorities (i.e. plebeians and patricians) are equal, it will lead, inevitably, to a power struggle. 113. **gratis**: free and, presumably, without merit. 114. **no more of that**: We may wonder, was it Menenius' idea, or is he protecting Cominius, who was consul when the creation of the tribunes was approved? 118. **my reasons**: He has already done so, but the reiteration hardens the tribunes against him still more. 119-24. **corn/ Was not our recompense...Did not deserve corn gratis**: There is a narrative problem here. In 1.1, the people demanded grain corn before the war; ergo, their so-called cowardice at Corioli is a moot point. It is possible that the corn was only given after the battle of Corioli. If so, then Martius is really being unfair, since the people not only rescued him in his recklessness, but also helped him, ultimately, to take the town. See 1.4.48-64, above. 128. **cause unborn**: An unmerited cause. 130. **beesom**: seeming, unreliable. 133. **true fear**: Martius refuses to recognize the possibility that the people might like a government that functions in its favor.

	The nature of our seats and make the rabble	135
	Call our cares fears; which will in time break ope	
	The locks o' th' Senate and bring in the crows	
	To peck the eagles.	
MENENIUS	Come, enough.	
BRUTUS	Enough, with over-measure.	
MARTIUS	No, take more!	
	What may be sworn by, both divine and human,	140
	Seal what I end withal! This double worship—	
	Where one part does disdain with cause, the other	
	Insult without all reason; where gentry, title, wisdom	
	Cannot conclude but by the yea and no	
	Of general ignorance—it must omit	145
	Real necessities, and give way the while	
	To unstable slightness. Purpose so barr'd, it follows	
	Nothing is done to purpose. Therefore, beseech you—	
	You that will be less fearful than discreet;	
	That love the fundamental part of state	150
	More than you doubt the change on't; that prefer	
	A noble life before a long, and wish	
	To jump a body with a dangerous physic	
	That's sure of death without it—at once pluck out	
	The multitudinous tongue; let them not lick	155
	The sweet which is their poison. Your dishonor	
	Mangles true judgment, and bereaves the state	
	Of that integrity which should become't,	
	Not having the power to do the good it would	
	For th' ill which doth control't.	
BRUTUS	Has said enough.	160
SICINUS	Has spoken like a traitor and shall answer	
	As traitors do.	

---

135. **rabble**: mob. 136. **cares fears**: Honest care will be misunderstood as weakness. 136-38. **break ope/The locks**: Open the way to insurrection. —**crows...eagles**: crows/plebeians; eagles/ patricians. Further, crows are carrion eaters that peck at the dead; eagles are predatory birds, hunters. 139. **over-measure**: This is too much. 142-43. **disdain with cause**: The patricians have cause to disdain the plebeians. —**the other/Insult without all reason**: The plebeians, in their unthinking demands, insult the ruling aristocrats. 145. **general ignorance**: The ignorance of the plebeians. 146-48. **Real necessities...Nothing is done to purpose**: Important, long terms matters will be put off for short-term gains. As a critique of democracy, this one is probably valid. 153. **dangerous physic**: poisonous medicine, more harmful than helpful. 154-55. **pluck out/ The multitudinous tongue**: A long rant that comes down to a reiteration of 3.1.97-104. 157. **bereaves**: takes from. 158. **Of that**: That quality of. 160. **th'ill which doth control't**: The disease/ill (the plebeians), which now (or inevitably will) control the state. See commentary at 1.3.98.

MARTIUS	Thou wretch, despite o'erwhelm thee!
	What should the people do with these bald tribunes?
	On whom depending, their obedience fails
	To th' greater bench. In a rebellion, 165
	When what's not meet, but what must be, was law,
	Then were they chosen. In a better hour,
	Let what is meet be said it must be meet,
	And throw their power i' th' dust.
BRUTUS	Manifest treason!
SICINUS	This a consul? No. 170
BRUTUS	The ædiles, ho!

Enter an Ædile.

	Let him be apprehended.
SICINUS	Go call the people, [*Exit Ædile*]
	in whose name myself
	Attach thee as a traitorous innovator,
	A foe to th' public weal. Obey, I charge thee,
	And follow to thine answer.
MARTIUS	Hence, old goat! 175
ALL [PATRICIANS]	We'll surety him.
COMINIUS	Aged sir, hands off.
MARTIUS	Hence, rotten thing! or I shall shake thy bones
	Out of thy garments.
SICINUS	Help, ye citizens!

Enter a rabble of Plebeians, with the Ædiles.

MENENIUS	On both sides more respect.
SICINUS	Here's he that would take from you all your power. 180
BRUTUS	Seize him, ædiles!
ALL [PLEBEIANS]	Down with him! down with him!

---

162. **despite o'erwhelm thee**: A curse on you! 163. **bald**: The tribunes may be bald, or it may suggest their naked, or exposed motives. 167. **Then were they chosen**: Martius argues that, since the posts of tribune were recreated during an insurrection, they are not legitimate parts of the government. See 1.1.198-205. 168. **what is meet be said**: Say what has to be said. 171. **ædiles**: Security, police. 173. **innovator**: instigator. 174. **public weal**: the people. 175. **old goat**: This, with a reference to "bald" (3.1.163) and "Aged sir" (3.1.176), suggests the tribunes' age. 176. **We'll surety him**: We'll post bail for him. There is no reason to arrest him; if there are charges, we will vouch for him. The fact that Sicinius disregards Cominius, the former consul of Rome, suggests that Martius' analysis of power may, in this instance, be correct. 179. **On both sides more respect**: More respectful of each other. Ironic, in that Menenius has also insulted the people. See 1.1.140-46.

2 SENATOR	Weapons, weapons, weapons!
	They all bustle about Martius, [crying]:
	Tribunes!—Patricians!—Citizens!—What, ho!—
	Sicinius!—Brutus!—Coriolanus!—Citizens! 185
ALL [PATRICIANS]	Peace, peace, peace! Stay, hold, peace!
MENENIUS	What is about to be? I am out of breath.
	Confusion's near. I cannot speak. You, Tribunes,
	Speak to th' people. Coriolanus, patience.
	Speak, good Sicinius.
SICINIUS	Hear me, people. Peace! 190
ALL [PLEBEIANS]	Let's hear our tribune. Peace! Speak, speak, speak!
SICINIUS	You are at point to lose your liberties.
	Martius would have all from you, Martius,
	Whom late you have nam'd for consul.
MENENIUS	Fie, fie, fie!
	This is the way to kindle, not to quench. 195
1 SENATOR	To unbuild the city and to lay all flat.
SICINIUS	What is the city but the people?
ALL [PLEBEIANS]	True!
	The people are the city.
BRUTUS	By the consent of all we were establish'd
	The people's magistrates.
ALL [PLEBEIANS]	You so remain. 200
MENENIUS	And so are like to do.
MARTIUS	That is the way to lay the city flat,
	To bring the roof to the foundation,
	And bury all which yet distinctly ranges
	In heaps and piles of ruin.
SICINIUS	This deserves death. 205
BRUTUS	Or let us stand to our authority
	Or let us lose it. We do here pronounce
	Upon the part o' th' people, in whose power
	We were elected theirs, Martius is worthy
	Of present death.

183. **Weapons**: As Martius predicted, sharing power turns into a struggle for power. See 3.1.117-38, above. 186. **hold**: hold back violence. 195. **kindle**: As in set the city on fire. See 4.3.17 and 4.6.137. 198. **all**: Not really. Menenius was absent. See 1.1.197, above. 201. **And so are like to do**: And so are likely to remain the people's magistrates/representatives. 202-05. **lay the city…ruin**: Kittredge follows the Folio of 1623 in attributing these lines to Cominius. Given Sicinius' reply, we must either think that Cominus is now also seen as an enemy of the people, or that the lines more properly belong to Coriolanus.

SICINUS	Therefore lay hold of him.	210
	Bear him to th' Rock Tarpeian and from thence	
	Into destruction cast him.	
BRUTUS	Ædiles, seize him!	
ALL [PLEBEIANS]	Yield, Martius, yield!	
MENENIUS	Hear me one word.	
	Beseech you, Tribunes, hear me but a word.	
ÆDILES	Peace, peace!	215
MENENIUS	[to Brutus] Be that you seem, truly your country's friend,	
	And temp'rately proceed to what you would	
	Thus violently redress.	
BRUTUS	Sir, those cold ways	
	That seem like prudent helps are very poisonous	
	Where the disease is violent.—Lay hands upon him	
	And bear him to the Rock. *Martius draws his sword.*	
MARTIUS	No, I'll die here.	
	There's some among you have beheld me fighting.	
	Come try upon yourselves what you have seen me.	
MENENIUS	Down with that sword! Tribunes, withdraw awhile.	
BRUTUS	Lay hands upon him.	
MENENIUS	Help Martius, help!	225
	You that be noble, help him, young and old!	
ALL [PLEBEIANS]	Down with him! down with him!	

In this mutiny the Tribunes, the Ædiles, and the People are beat in.

MENENIUS	Go, get you to your house! Be gone, away!	
	All will be naught else.	
2 SENATOR	Get you gone.	
MARTIUS	Stand fast!	
	We have as many friends as enemies.	230
MENENIUS	Shall it be put to that?	
1 SENATOR	The gods forbid!	

---

211. **Rock Tarpeian**: Infamous place of execution for traitors. 212. **Into destruction**: Hurl off a cliff, in this case, the Tarpeian Rock. 214. **Beseech you**: With patience, please. 216-18. **Be that you seem... redress**: If you are truly interested in the people's good, you will not turn so promptly to violence. In short, let's talk about this. 219-20. **prudent...poisonous...disease is violent**: Desperate times don't call for half measures. Illness metaphor echoes Martius' own assessment of Rome at 3.1.153-56, above. See also 1.3.98. 225. **him**: Menenius. A sign of cowardice? Instead of attacking Martius, they seize an old man. 229. **naught**: ruined.

I prithee, noble friend, home to thy house.
Leave us to cure this cause.

MENENIUS   For 'tis a sore upon us
you cannot tent yourself. Be gone, beseech you.

COMINIUS   Come, sir, along with us.   235

MARTIUS   I would they were barbarians, as they are,
Though in Rome litter'd; not Romans, as they are not,
Though calv'd i' th' porch o' th' Capitol.

MENENIUS   Be gone.
Put not your worthy rage into your tongue.   240
One time will owe another.

MARTIUS   On fair ground
I could beat forty of them.

MENENIUS   I could myself
Take up a brace o' th' best of them; yea, the two tribunes.

COMINIUS   But now 'tis odds beyond arithmetic,
And manhood is call'd foolery when it stands   245
Against a falling fabric. Will you hence
Before the tag return? whose rage doth rend
Like interrupted waters, and o'erbear
What they are us'd to bear.

MENENIUS   Pray you be gone.
I'll try whether my old wit be in request   250
With those that have but little. This must be patch'd
With cloth of any color.

COMINIUS   Nay, come away.
                  Exeunt Martius and Cominius, [with others].

PATRICIAN   This man has marr'd his fortune.

MENENIUS   His nature is too noble for the world.
He would not flatter Neptune for his trident   255
Or Jove for's power to thunder. His heart's his mouth;
What his breast forges, that his tongue must vent,

231. **home**: go home. 236. **barbarians**: Therefore worthy of slaughter. 237. **litter'd**: As in an animal litter, born. 240. **worthy**: justifiable. 241. **fair ground**: good fighting surface, flat. 243. **brace**: the people compared to a flock of geese. 245. **foolery**: A tacit critique of Martius' attack at Corioli? See 1.4.48-64, above. 246. **fabric**: See tag/ragtag, in next line. 247. **tag**: ragtag mob. 248. **waters**: Compare the violence of the surging mob to Martius himself at 2.2.295, above. 250. **my old wit**: Menenius did, after all, stop a rebellion when he told the mob the story of the belly at 1.1.79-138. 251. **patch'd**: a quick, temporary fix. 252. **Nay**: Cominius convincing Martius to go with him. Clearly, Martius prefers to stand and to fight. 253. **marr'd**: ruined. 255. **Neptune**: God of the sea. 256. **Jove**: God of the heavens and, thus, thunder. 257. **tongue must vent**: Martius is impolite.

And being angry does forget that ever
He heard the name of death.

A noise within.

Here's goodly work!

PATRICIAN   I would they were abed!   260

MENENIUS   I would they were in Tiber! What the vengeance,
Could he not speak 'em fair?

Enter Brutus and Sicinius with the Rabble again.

SICINIUS   Where is this viper
That would depopulate the city and
Be every man himself?

MENENIUS   You worthy Tribunes—

SICINIUS   He shall be thrown down the Tarpeian Rock   265
With rigorous hands. He hath resisted law,
And therefore law shall scorn him further trial
Than the severity of the public power,
Which he so sets at naught.

1 CITIZEN   He shall well know
The noble tribunes are the people's mouths,   270
And we their hands.

ALL [PLEBEIANS]   He shall, sure on't!

MENENIUS   Sir, sir—

SICINIUS   Peace!

MENENIUS   Do not cry havoc where you should but hunt
With modest warrant.

SICINIUS   Sir, how comes't that you
Have holp to make this rescue?

MENENIUS   Hear me speak.   275
As I do know the consul's worthiness,
So can I name his faults.

<hr>

258-59. **forget…the name of death**: Once roused, Martius is fearless. 260. **goodly work**: Ironic commentary on the mob, which is out for blood. 261. **in Tiber**: The nearby river; drowned. 262. **he**: Martius. The tribunes are not seen as the sole cause of the riot. 266. **rigorous**: unfeeling, without pity. 267. **scorn him further trial**: reject any further discussion of the matter. 271. **we their hands**: The inference here is that the mob will kill Martius, not the ædiles; the act, therefore, dispenses with the forms and niceties of law and order. The image of the common folk killing Martius foreshadows 5.6.128-29. 273. **cry havoc…modest warrant**: Menenius again calls for calm. 275. **holp**: hope.

| SICINUS | Consul? What consul? |

MENENIUS   The consul Coriolanus.

BRUTUS   He consul?

ALL [Plebeians]   No, no, no, no, no!

MENENIUS   If, by the tribunes' leave, and yours, good people,   280
I may be heard, I would crave a word or two,
The which shall turn you to no further harm
Than so much loss of time.

SICINUS   Speak briefly then,
For we are peremptory to dispatch
This viperous traitor. To eject him hence   285
Were but our danger, and to keep him here
Our certain death. Therefore it is decreed
He dies tonight.

MENENIUS   Now the good gods forbid
That our renowned Rome, whose gratitude
Towards her deserved children is enroll'd   290
In Jove's own book, like an unnatural dam
Should now eat up her own!

SICINUS   He's a disease that must be cut away.

MENENIUS   O, he's a limb that has but a disease:
Mortal to cut it off; to cure it, easy.   295
What has he done to Rome that's worthy death?
Killing our enemies, the blood he hath lost
(Which, I dare vouch, is more than that he hath,
By many an ounce) he dropp'd it for his country;
And what is left, to lose it by his country   300
Were to us all that do't and suffer it
A brand to th' end o' th' world.

SICINUS   This is clean kam.

---

277. **What consul**: The tribunes reject the vote already taken. 280. **leave**: permission. 281. **a word or two**: Menenius is trying to stall them; see commentaries for 1.1.73-147, above. 284-88. **preemptory to dispatch…tonight**: Our minds are fixed. He must die tonight. 291. **Jove's own book**: Related to the biblical story of God recording your deeds for later judgment. Malachi 3:16 (King James Version): "Then they that feared the LORD spake often one to another: and the LORD hearkened, and heard it, and a book of remembrance was written before him for them that feared the LORD, and that thought upon his name." 291-92. **unnatural dam…eat up her own**: Ironic, Cronus/Saturn tried to eat his son Zeus/Jove and Zeus/Jove himself ate his lover Metis, who was pregnant. Later, Zeus's head cracked open and out sprang a fully armored Athena—or Minerva in the Roman myths. 294-95. **limb that has but a disease:/Mortal to cut it off**: Menenius agrees that Martius is a problem, but that seeking his death goes too far. See disease images at 1.3.98. 302. **brand**: a stain, mark, sin, as in Cain, who was branded for the murder of his brother Abel. —**kam**: nonsense.

BRUTUS	Merely awry. When he did love his country, It honor'd him.	
MENENIUS	The service of the foot, Being once gangren'd, is not then respected For what before it was.	305
BRUTUS	We'll hear no more. Pursue him to his house and pluck him thence, Lest his infection, being of catching nature, Spread further.	
MENENIUS	One word more, one word! This tiger-footed rage, when it shall find The harm of unscann'd swiftness, will (too late) Tie leaden pounds to's heels. Proceed by process, Lest parties (as he is belov'd) break out And sack great Rome with Romans.	310
BRUTUS	If it were so—	
SICINUS	What do ye talk? Have we not had a taste of his obedience— Our ædiles smote? ourselves resisted? Come!	315
MENENIUS	Consider this: he has been bred i' th' wars Since 'a could draw a sword, and is ill-school'd In bolted language; meal and bran together He throws without distinction. Give me leave, I'll go to him and undertake to bring him Where he shall answer by a lawful form (In peace) to his utmost peril.	320
1 SENATOR	Noble Tribunes, It is the humane way. The other course Will prove too bloody, and the end of it Unknown to the beginning.	325
SICINUS	Noble Menenius, Be you then as the people's officer. Masters, lay down your weapons.	

303. **Merely awry**: Off the mark. 304. **service of the foot**: Menenius is back to his tale of the belly metaphor. Ironically, the foot contains the "great toe." See 1.1.140-41, above. 307. **pluck**: drag. 308. **infection**: In this case, a hatred of the people. 311. **unscann'd swiftness**: rash, hasty actions. 312. **Proceed by process**: By the courts of law. 314. **sack**: pillage. 316. **his**: Martius'. 317. **smote**: struck violently. 320. **bolted language**: bolted down, constrained, therefore polite. —**meal and bran**: coarse and soft food; Martius deals with them, as with words, indiscriminately. 323. **lawful form**: Due process. 327. **Unknown to the beginning**: If you kill him like this there may be calamitous ramifications. 329. **lay down your weapons**: The tribunes seemingly agree to the rule of law, but do not disperse their faction. In other words, mob violence remains an option and a threat.

BRUTUS   Go not home.

SICINUS   Meet on the market place. We'll attend you there,   330
Where if you bring not Martius, we'll proceed
In our first way.

MENENIUS   I'll bring him to you. [*To the Senators*] Let me
Desire your company. He must come, or what
Is worst will follow.

1 SENATOR   Pray you, let's to him.   *Exeunt omnes.*

SCENE II. [*A room in the house of Coriolanus.*]

Enter Martius with Nobles.

MARTIUS   Let them pull all about mine ears; present me
Death on the wheel or at wild horses' heels;
Or pile ten hills on the Tarpeian Rock,
That the precipitation might down stretch
Below the beam of sight—yet will I still   5
Be thus to them.

NOBLE   You do the nobler.

MARTIUS   I muse my mother
Does not approve me further, who was wont
To call them woollen vassals, things created
To buy and sell with groats, to show bare heads   10
In congregations, to yawn, be still, and wonder
When one but of my ordinance stood up
To speak of peace or war.

Enter Volumnia.

I talk of you.
Why did you wish me milder? Would you have me
False to my nature? Rather say, I play   15
The man I am.

SCENE II.
1. **pull all**: destroy all. 2. **wheel or at wild horses' heels**: Modes of execution. The wheel involved the systematic breaking of bones; arms and legs were tied to four wild horses, who then were whipped until the victim's body was torn to pieces. 4. **precipitation**: What falls from heaven; in this case, Martius' body, falling from the Tarpeian Rock. 7. **muse**: wonder why. 9-13. **woollen vassels, things created/...peace or war**: Volumnia has schooled Martius to think of the people as worthless and mindless. 14. **Why did you wish me milder**: Why did you want me to speak to the people with less contempt? 15. **False to my nature**: Yet, as Martius admits, he has merely recited what his mother feels; his nature is, in effect, her nature. See 2.1.178-80, above.

VOLUMNIA   O, sir, sir, sir!
                    I would have had you put your power well on
                    Before you had worn it out.

MARTIUS   Let't go.

MENENIUS   You might have been enough the man you are
                    With striving less to be so. Lesser had been   20
                    The thwarting of your dispositions, if
                    You had not show'd them how ye were dispos'd
                    Ere they lack'd power to cross you.

MARTIUS   Let them hang.

VOLUMNIA   Ay, and burn too!

                    Enter Menenius with the Senators.

MENENIUS   Come, come, you have been too rough, something too rough.
                    You must return and mend it.

SENATOR   There's no remedy,   26
                    Unless, by not so doing, our good city
                    Cleave in the midst and perish.

VOLUMNIA   Pray be counsell'd.
                    I have a heart as little apt as yours,
                    But yet a brain that leads my use of anger   30
                    To better vantage.

MENENIUS   Well said, noble woman!
                    Before he should thus stoop to th' herd, but that
                    The violent fit o' th' time craves it as physic
                    For the whole state, I would put mine armor on,
                    Which I can scarcely bear.

MARTIUS   What must I do?   35

MENENIUS   Return to th' tribunes.

MARTIUS   Well, what then? what then?

16-17. **put your power well on/Before you had worn it out**: You should have remained quiet until you were fully invested as consul. Then you could have done or spoken as you liked. Yet, even though he was contemptuous, Martius did receive the people's votes and was invested by the Senate. By the rule of law, then, he is already consul. 19-22. **enough the man you are/...had not show'd them how ye were dispos'd**: You might have been a man, and, thus, true to yourself, if you were not so vocal. Note that Martius has hitherto been modest in victory. The original text assigns these lines to Volumnia, yet the measured tenor is more in keeping with Menenius, who has called for calm throughout 3.1. The same tenor is used in his speech at 3.2.25-26. Further, note Volumnia's next speech at 3.2.26, which is more in keeping with her rough exterior. 28. **Cleave**: split, as in civil war factions. 29. **apt**: willing. 31. **vantage**: advantage. 33. **time craves it as physic**: Medical metaphor, as in 3.1.98. In essence, desperate times, desperate measure. 34. **put mine armor on**: Menenius might be a tough old man, or there might be some false bravado here.

MENENIUS	Repent what you have spoke.
MARTIUS	For them? I cannot do it to the gods.
	Must I then do't to them?
VOLUMNIA	You are too absolute;

Though therein you can never be too noble,   40
But when extremities speak. I have heard you say,
Honor and policy, like unsever'd friends,
I' th' war do grow together. Grant that, and tell me,
In peace what each of them by th' other lose,
That they combine not there.

MARTIUS	Tush, tush!
MENENIUS	A good demand.
VOLUMNIA	If it be honor in your wars to seem 46

The same you are not,—which, for your best ends,
You adopt your policy,—how is it less or worse
That it shall hold companionship in peace
With honor, as in war; since that to both   50
It stands in like request?

MARTIUS	Why force you this?
VOLUMNIA	Because that now it lies you on to speak

To th' people, not by your own instruction,
Nor by th' matter which your heart prompts you,
But with such words that are but roted in   55
Your tongue, though but bastards and syllables
Of no allowance to your bosom's truth.
Now, this no more dishonors you at all
Than to take in a town with gentle words
Which else would put you to your fortune and   60
The hazard of much blood.
I would dissemble with my nature where
My fortunes and my friends at stake requir'd
I should do so in honor. I am in this
Your wife, your son, these senators, the nobles;   65
And you will rather show our general louts

38-39. **I cannot do it to the gods./Must I then do't to them**: If I can't apologize to the gods, how can I do it to these subhumans? See 1.1.243. —**absolute**: extreme. 42-50. **Honor and policy...as in war**: If you can use subterfuge in war, why not in politics? 51. **force**: argue. 52. **now it lies you on**: now it lies in you. 55-56. **roted in/Your tongue**: Words memorized, not from the heart. 57. **bosom's truth**: Heart's true, sincere feelings. 59. **take in a town with gentle words**: From what we have seen, this tactic is not in Martius' arsenal. 60. **fortune**: chance. 61. **hazard**: risk. 62. **dissemble**: hide, lie. 64. **I am in this**: In this matter, I speak on behalf of. 66. **general louts**: Joe Six-Pack types.

How you can frown than spend a fawn upon 'em
For the inheritance of their loves and safeguard
Of what that want might ruin.

MENENIUS   Noble lady!
Come, go with us. Speak fair. You may salve so,   70
Not what is dangerous present, but the loss
Of what is past.

VOLUMNIA   I prithee now, my son,
Go to them, with this bonnet in thy hand;
And thus far having stretch'd it (here be with them),
Thy knee bussing the stones (for in such business   75
Action is eloquence, and the eyes of th' ignorant
More learned than the ears), waving thy head,
Which often, thus, correcting thy stout heart,
Now humble as the ripest mulberry
That will not hold the handling—say to them   80
Thou art their soldier, and, being bred in broils,
Hast not the soft way which, thou dost confess,
Were fit for thee to use, as they to claim,
In asking their good loves; but thou wilt frame
Thyself (forsooth) hereafter theirs, so far   85
As thou hast power and person.

MENENIUS   This but done
Even as she speaks, why, their hearts were yours!
For they have pardons, being ask'd, as free
As words to little purpose.

VOLUMNIA   Prithee now,
Go, and be rul'd; although I know thou hadst rather   90
Follow thine enemy in a fiery gulf
Than flatter him in a bower.

                    Enter Cominius.

                          Here is Cominius.

COMINIUS   I have been i' th' market place; and, sir, 'tis fit

	You make strong party, or defend yourself
	By calmness or by absence. All's in anger. 95
MENENIUS	Only fair speech.
COMINIUS	I think 'twill serve, if he
	Can thereto frame his spirit.
VOLUMNIA	He must and will.
	Prithee now, say you will, and go about it.
MARTIUS	Must I go show them my unbarb'd sconce? Must I
	With my base tongue give to my noble heart 100
	A lie that it must bear? Well, I will do't.
	Yet, were there but this single plot to lose,
	This mould of Martius, they to dust should grind it
	And throw't against the wind. To th' market place!
	You have put me now to such a part which never 105
	I shall discharge to th' life.
COMINIUS	Come, come, we'll prompt you.
VOLUMNIA	I prithee now, sweet son, as thou hast said
	My praises made thee first a soldier, so,
	To have my praise for this, perform a part
	Thou hast not done before.
MARTIUS	Well, I must do't. 110
	Away, my disposition, and possess me
	Some harlot's spirit! My throat of war be turn'd,
	Which quier'd with my drum, into a pipe
	Small as an eunuch or the virgin voice
	That babies lulls asleep! The smiles of knaves 115
	Tent in my cheeks, and schoolboys' tears take up
	The glasses of my sight! A beggar's tongue
	Make motion through my lips, and my arm'd knees,
	Who bow'd but in my stirrup, bend like his
	That hath receiv'd an alms! I will not do't, 120
	Lest I surcease to honor mine own truth

94-95. **strong party...absence**: Not go alone, or not go at all. 99. **unbarb'd sconce**: Cap in hand, nothing on my head. 100. **base**: without honor. 102-03. **single plot to lose,/...they to dust should grind it**: Frankly, I'd rather die than do as you ask, but I'll do it. 105-06. **You have put me now to such a part which never/I shall discharge to th'life**: I'll never do this convincingly. 106. **prompt**: As in an actor's prompt. We'll help you. 108. **my praises made thee first a soldier**: Volumnia concedes that all Martius has done, he has done to please her. She may be overvaluing herself here. Rome is a martial society. 112. **harlot's spirit**: Sell yourself like a prostitute for the consulship. 113. **quier'd**: sang, as in choir. 114. **Small as an eunuch**: Or, one might say a girl. See 1.3.5 and 2.2.87, above. 115. **knaves**: the unworthy, fools and thieves. 116. **schoolboys' tears**: Schoolboys acting in plays, anticipates 5.6.100.

	And by my body's action teach my mind	
	A most inherent baseness.	
VOLUMNIA	At thy choice then.	
	To beg of thee, it is my more dishonor	
	Than thou of them. Come all to ruin! Let	125
	Thy mother rather feel thy pride than fear	
	Thy dangerous stoutness; for I mock at death	
	With as big heart as thou. Do as thou list.	
	Thy valiantness was mine, thou suck'st it from me;	
	But owe thy pride thyself.	
MARTIUS	Pray be content.	130
	Mother, I am going to the market place.	
	Chide me no more. I'll mountebank their loves,	
	Cog their hearts from them, and come home belov'd	
	Of all the trades in Rome. Look, I am going.	
	Commend me to my wife. I'll return consul,	135
	Or never trust to what my tongue can do	
	I' th' way of flattery further.	
VOLUMNIA	Do your will. *Exit.*	
COMINIUS	Away! The tribunes do attend you. Arm yourself	
	To answer mildly, for they are prepar'd	
	With accusations, as I hear, more strong	140
	Than are upon you yet.	
MARTIUS	The word is "mildly." Pray you let us go.	
	Let them accuse me by invention; I	
	Will answer in mine honor.	
MENENIUS	Ay, but mildly.	
MARTIUS	Well, mildly be it then—mildly.	145

Exeunt.

122-23. **my body's action teach my mind/ A most inherent baseness**: I.e., If I go through the motions, I will be poisoning the purity of my mind. —**At thy choice**: Do as you like—a bit of reverse psychology from Volumnia. 124-25. **my more dishonor/Than thou of them**: For Volumnia to beg Martius is worse/more dishonorable than Martius to beg the people. She is voicing her contempt for her son. Of course, he capitulates. 128. **Do as thou list**: Do as you like, feigning indifference. 130. **Pray be content**: I promise, I'll do it. 132. **Chide**: Scold. —**mountebank**: Perform like a mountebank, a conman. 133. **Cog**: Steal. 134. **trades**: working class. 137. **Do your will**: Do as you like, feigning indifference. 138. **Arm yourself**: Cominius suggests that to be liked is like going to war; you need a plan. 141. **Than are upon you yet**: Than you have hitherto heard. 143. **invention**: Without substance, lies.

SCENE III. [*Rome. The Forum.*]

Enter Sicinius and Brutus.

BRUTUS   In this point charge him home, that he affects
Tyrannical power. If he evade us there,
Enforce him with his envy to the people,
And that the spoil got on the Antiates
Was ne'er distributed.

Enter an Ædile.

What, will he come?   5

ÆDILE   He's coming.

BRUTUS   How accompanied?

ÆDILE   With old Menenius and those senators
That always favor'd him.

SICINUS   Have you a catalogue
Of all the voices that we have procur'd
Set down by th' poll?

ÆDILE   I have; 'tis ready.   10

SICINUS   Have you collected them by tribes?

ÆDILE   I have.

SICINUS   Assemble presently the people hither;
And when they hear me say "It shall be so
I' th' right and strength o' th' commons," be it either
For death, for fine, or banishment, then let them,   15
If I say fine, cry "Fine!"—if death, cry "Death!"
Insisting on the old prerogative
And power i' th' truth o' th' cause.

ÆDILE   I shall inform them.

BRUTUS   And when such time they have begun to cry,
Let them not cease, but with a din confus'd   20
Enforce the present execution
Of what we chance to sentence.

ÆDILE   Very well.

SCENE III
1. **charge him home**: Press your advantage, suggesting that the tribunes also see this meeting with Martius as a tactical skirmish. 3. **Enforce him**: Accuse him. 4. **the spoil**: war loot; obviously a lie, since Martius cares nothing for such trifles. See 1.5.1-4, above. 4. **Antiates**: See 1.6.53, above. 8. **catalogue**: list. 17. **old prerogative**: established rights and powers. Yet these prerogatives are not so old. See 1.1.198-204, above. 20. **din confus'd**: crowd noise. 21. **Enforce**: Demand. —**present**: immediate. 22. **chance**: decide.

| SICINUS | Make them be strong, and ready for this hint |
| | When we shall hap to give't them. |

BRUTUS   Go about it.   [*Exit Ædile.*]
　　Put him to choler straight. He hath been us'd   25
　　Ever to conquer, and to have his worth
　　Of contradiction. Being once chaf'd, he cannot
　　Be rein'd again to temperance; then he speaks
　　What's in his heart, and that is there which looks
　　With us to break his neck.

Enter Martius, Menenius, and Cominius, with others [of their party].

SICINUS   Well, here he comes.   30

MENENIUS   Calmly, I do beseech you.

MARTIUS   Ay, as an hostler, that for th' poorest piece
　　Will bear the knave by th' volume. Th' honor'd gods
　　Keep Rome in safety, and the chairs of justice
　　Supplied with worthy men! plant love among's!   35
　　Throng our large temples with the shows of peace
　　And not our streets with war!

1 SENATOR   Amen, amen.

MENENIUS   A noble wish.

Enter the Ædile, with the Plebeians.

SICINUS   Draw near, ye people.

ÆDILE   List to your tribunes. Audience! Peace, I say!   40

MARTIUS   First hear me speak.

BOTH TRIBUNES   Well, say. Peace, ho!

MARTIUS   Shall I be charg'd no further than this present?
　　Must all determine here?

SICINUS   I do demand
　　If you submit you to the people's voices,
　　Allow their officers, and are content   45
　　To suffer lawful censure for such faults
　　As shall be prov'd upon you.

---

24. **hap**: will likely. 25. **choler**: anger. 25-26. **hath been us'd/Ever to conquer**: Coriolanus is not one to back down from a fight. 27. **chaf'd**: Irritated, like a bull. 28. **rein'd again to temperance**: made calm again. 29-30. **there which looks/ With us to break his neck**: His facial expressions of contempt will doom him to execution. 32-37. **Ay, as an hostler…not our streets with war**: Like a servant, ready to do anyone's bidding for any price. The rest of the speech seems to be a recitation of political platitudes, voiced contemptuously. The Senator and Menenius, willing to wring what concessions they can out of him, ignore his belly-aching. 40. **List**: Listen. 45. **content**: agreed. A key point: Martius agrees that the court is lawful. See 3.1.323 and 3.3.47.

MARTIUS	I am content.
MENENIUS	Lo, citizens, he says he is content.
	The warlike service he has done, consider. Think
	Upon the wounds his body bears, which show 50
	Like graves i' th' holy churchyard.
MARTIUS	Scratches with briers,
	Scars to move laughter only.
MENENIUS	Consider further,
	That when he speaks not like a citizen,
	You find him like a soldier. Do not take
	His rougher accents for malicious sounds, 55
	But, as I say, such as become a soldier
	Rather than envy you.
COMINIUS	[to Martius] Well, well, no more.
MARTIUS	What is the matter,
	That, being pass'd for consul with full voice,
	I am so dishonor'd that the very hour 60
	You take it off again?
SICINUS	Answer to us.
MARTIUS	Say then. 'Tis true, I ought so.
SICINUS	We charge you that you have contriv'd to take
	From Rome all season'd office and to wind
	Yourself into a power tyrannical, 65
	For which you are a traitor to the people.
MARTIUS	How? traitor?
MENENIUS	Nay, temperately! Your promise.
MARTIUS	The fires i' th' lowest hell fold-in the people!†
	Call me their traitor, thou injurious tribune?
	Within thine eyes sat twenty thousand deaths, 70
	In thy hands clutch'd as many millions, in
	Thy lying tongue both numbers, I would say
	'Thou liest' unto thee with a voice as free
	As I do pray the gods.
SICINUS	Mark you this, people?

---

51. **Like graves**: Each wound signifies an enemy buried. Echoing 2.1.107, above. —**Scratches with briers**: Scratches, incidental wounds. 54. **like a soldier**: Too honest to be a politician. See Volumnia's advice at 3.2.81-84, above. 59. **pass'd**: accepted. 64. **season'd office**: customary power. Ironic, since the tribunes' attempt to try Martius exceeds their customary power. 67. **temperately**: calmly. 70. **Within**: If within.

†   Hatred of the mob: Robert Burr's Coriolanus (dir. Joseph Papp; Delacorte Theatre, NYC, 1965) could not "conceal his contempt for the rabble; he cannot bear to pretend; he is by his hot-blooded nature ... all restlessness and impatience.... His roaring at the crowd is a cry of wrath at himself, the anger of a man who should have known better than to let himself be talked into a try for the consulship" (Howard Taubman, *New York Times*, July 15, 1965).

ALL [PLEBEIANS]	To th' Rock, to th' Rock with him!	
SICINUS	Peace!	75
	We need not put new matter to his charge.	
	What you have seen him do and heard him speak,	
	Beating your officers, cursing yourselves,	
	Opposing laws with strokes, and here defying	
	Those whose great power must try him—even this,	80
	So criminal and in such capital kind,	
	Deserves th' extremest death.	
BRUTUS	But since he hath	
	Serv'd well for Rome—	
MARTIUS	What do you prate of service?	
BRUTUS	I talk of that that know it.	
MARTIUS	You?	85
MENENIUS	Is this the promise that you made your mother?	
COMINIUS	Know, I pray you—	
MARTIUS	I'll know no further.	
	Let them pronounce the steep Tarpeian death,	
	Vagabond exile, flaying, pent to linger	
	But with a grain a day—I would not buy	90
	Their mercy at the price of one fair word,	
	Nor check my courage for what they can give,	
	To have't with saying "Good morrow."	
SICINUS	For that he has	
	(As much as in him lies) from time to time	
	Envied against the people, seeking means	95
	To pluck away their power; as now at last	
	Given hostile strokes, and that not in the presence	
	Of dreaded justice but on the ministers	
	That do distribute it—in the name o' th' people	
	And in the power of us the tribunes, we	100
	(Ev'n from this instant) banish him our city,	
	In peril of precipitation	
	From off the Rock Tarpeian, never more	
	To enter our Rome gates. I' th' people's name,	
	I say it shall be so.	105

75. **Rock**: The Tarpeian Rock; see 3.1.211. 76. **new matter**: new charges. 79. **strokes**: violence. 83. **prate**: talk, babble, prattle. 87. **know no further**: In other words, no longer listen to Brutus talk of what he supposedly knows. Since Martius thinks the tribunes and the people themselves are cowardly, he is offended by what looks to be a sudden recitation of his victories. 88-93. **Let them pronounce..."Good morrow."**: In other words, I'll not beg their mercy, even if it costs me next to nothing. 96. **pluck**: remove. —**as now at last**: and now, as seen recently.

ALL [PLEBEIANS]	It shall be so! it shall be so! Let him away! He's banish'd, and it shall be so!
COMINIUS	Hear me, my masters and my common friends!
SICINUS	He's sentenc'd. No more hearing.
COMINIUS	Let me speak.

COMINIUS (cont.)
I have been consul, and can show for Rome   110
Her enemies' marks upon me. I do love
My country's good with a respect more tender,
More holy and profound, than mine own life,
My dear wive's estimate, her womb's increase
And treasure of my loins. Then if I would   115
Speak that—

SICINUS   We know your drift. Speak what?

BRUTUS
There's no more to be said, but he is banish'd,
As enemy to the people and his country.
It shall be so.

ALL [PLEBEIANS]   It shall be so! it shall be so!

MARTIUS
You common cry of curs, whose breath I hate   120
As reek o' th' rotten fens, whose loves I prize
As the dead carcasses of unburied men
That do corrupt my air, I banish you!
And here remain with your uncertainty.
Let every feeble rumor shake your hearts!   125
Your enemies with nodding of their plumes
Fan you into despair! Have the power still
To banish your defenders, till at length
Your ignorance (which finds not till it feels,
Making not reservation of yourselves,   130
Still your own foes) deliver you, as most
Abated captives, to some nation
That won you without blows! Despising
For you the city, thus I turn my back.
There is a world elsewhere.   *Exeunt Martius, Cominius,*
                    [Menenius,] with [the other Patricians].

---

108. **masters**: The language suggests Cominius is now wooing the tribunes as equals. 111. **marks upon me**: Cominus refers to his own display of battlescars, as part of his ritual induction as consul. 114. **dear wive's estimate**: I love Rome more than my wife. See commentary at 1.1.215. 120. **curs**: dogs. 121. **fens**: swamps. 123. **corrupt my air**: Objectionable words compared to unwholesome, diseased air. See commentary at 1.3.98. —**I banish you**: Martius will leave, but on his own terms. 126. **nodding of their plumes**: The bobbing of army helmets as they march on Rome. 127-32. **Have...captives, to some nation**: Continue to do as you have done, and you will be prisoners of your enemies.

ÆDILE	The people's enemy is gone, is gone!	136

They all shout and throw up their caps.

ALL	Our enemy is banish'd! He is gone. Hoo! hoo!	

SICINUS	Go see him out at gates and follow him	
	As he hath follow'd you, with all despite;	
	Give him deserv'd vexation. Let a guard	140
	Attend us through the city.	

| ALL | Come, come, let's see him out at gates! Come! | |
| | The gods preserve our noble tribunes! Come!   *Exeunt.* | |

ACT IV

SCENE I. [*Rome. At a gate of the city.*]

Enter Martius, Volumnia, Virgilia, Menenius, Cominius,
with the young Nobility of Rome.

MARTIUS	Come, leave your tears. A brief farewell. The beast	
	With many heads butts me away. Nay, mother,	
	Where is your ancient courage?† You were us'd	
	To say extremity was the trier of spirits;	
	That common chances common men could bear;	5
	That when the sea was calm, all boats alike	
	Show'd mastership in floating; fortune's blows	
	When most struck home, being gentle wounded craves	
	A noble cunning. You were us'd to load me	
	With precepts that would make invincible	10
	The heart that conn'd them.	

138-39. **follow him...with all despite**: Compare to Martius' return to Rome, marked with great fanfare. See 2.1.142 sd., above. 143. **preserve**: defend, bless.
ACT IV. SCENE I.
1-2. **The beast/With many heads**: The multitudes, compared to the Hydra; see 2.3.9, above. 3. **ancient**: long-known. 4. **extremity was the trier of spirits**: In other words, that which does not kill you makes you strong. 5. **common chances common man could bear**: True heroism is only found in adversity; grace under pressure. 10. **precepts**: Wise sayings. 11. **conn'd**: studied.

---

† Attempting to please his mother: During a 1992 Chichester Theatre production (dir. Tim Supple), Martius (Kenneth Branagh) crawled away on hands and knees (Irving Wardle, *The Independent on Sunday*, May 17, 1992); his mother (Judi Dench) was a "domestic tyrant with the heart and stomach of a lion. ... Coriolanus is bound to her because he recognizes a fellow spirit" (Paul Taylor, *The Independent*, May 15, 1992).

VIRGILIA	O heavens! O heavens!
MARTIUS	Nay, I prithee, woman—
VOLUMNIA	Now the red pestilence strike all trades in Rome,
	And occupations perish!
MARTIUS	What, what, what!

I shall be lov'd when I am lack'd. Nay, mother,   15
Resume that spirit when you were wont to say,
If you had been the wife of Hercules,
Six of his labors you'ld have done, and sav'd
Your husband so much sweat. Cominius,
Droop not; adieu. Farewell, my wife, my mother.   20
I'll do well yet. Thou old and true Menenius,
Thy tears are salter than a younger man's
And venomous to thine eyes. My (sometime) General,
I have seen thee stern, and thou hast oft beheld
Heart-hard'ning spectacles. Tell these sad women   25
'Tis fond to wail inevitable strokes,
As 'tis to laugh at 'em. My mother, you wot well
My hazards still have been your solace; and
Believe't not lightly—though I go alone,
Like to a lonely dragon, that his fen   30
Makes fear'd and talk'd of more than seen—your son
Will or exceed the common or be caught
With cautelous baits and practice.

VOLUMNIA	My first son,

Whither wilt thou go? Take good Cominius
With thee awhile. Determine on some course   35
More than a wild exposture to each chance
That starts i' th' way before thee.

VIRGILIA	O the gods!
COMINIUS	I'll follow thee a month, devise with thee

Where thou shalt rest, that thou mayst hear of us,

---

13. **red pestilence**: typhus, a common infection among prisoners. In 1577, 300 died of the epidemic in Oxford. 15. **lack'd**: not around. 18. **Six of his labors you'ld have done**: Hercules' twelve labors, a sign of Volumnia's Amazonian nature. Ironic, in that the twelve labors were penance for Hercules' slaying of his wife, Megara, and their three children. A death-wish for her son? 20. **my wife, my mother**: The closeness of wife and mother in the address may suggest some Oedipal anxiety. See commentary at 1.3.2. 22. **salter**: Due to a lack of water; a Renaissance medical concept that older people were drier than younger people. 25. **Heart-hard'ning**: Cruel. 26. **fond**: silly. **—strokes**: difficulties, torture, pain. 27. **wot**: know. 28. **hazards**: battles. **—solace**: See 1.3.108. 30. **fen**: dragon's lair; see also 4.7.23 and 5.4.11. 33. **cautelous baits**: dangerous traps. That is, Martius will only be slayed by political turmoil, not by arms. **—first**: best, though it is possible she had another child. 36. **wild exposture**: Exposure to the wilds, wandering, homeless. 38. **devise**: plan.

And we of thee. So, if the time thrust forth   40
A cause for thy repeal, we shall not send
O'er the vast world to seek a single man
And lose advantage, which doth ever cool
I' th' absence of the needer.

MARTIUS   Fare ye well.
Thou hast years upon thee, and thou art too full   45
Of the wars' surfeits to go rove with one
That's yet unbruis'd. Bring me but out at gate.
Come, my sweet wife, my dearest mother, and
My friends of noble touch. When I am forth,
Bid me farewell, and smile. I pray you come.   50
While I remain above the ground, you shall
Hear from me still, and never of me aught
But what is like me formerly.

MENENIUS   That's worthily
As any ear can hear. Come, let's not weep.
If I could shake off but one seven years   55
From these old arms and legs, by the good gods,
I'ld with thee, every foot.

MARTIUS   Give me thy hand.
Come.   *Exeunt.*

SCENE II. [*Rome. A street near the gate.*]

Enter the two Tribunes, Sicinius and Brutus, with the Ædile.

SICINIUS   Bid them all home. He's gone, and we'll no further.
The nobility are vex'd, whom we see have sided
In his behalf.

BRUTUS   Now we have shown our power,

---

40. **if the time thrust forth**: If in the future. 43. **advantage**: of time and men searching for Martius. 43-44. **cool/I'th' absence of the needer**: loss of passion, interest. Out of sight, out of mind. 45. **Thou hast years upon thee**: The first indication that Cominius is not a young man. Might these words have been meant for Menenius? See Menenius's wish to go with Martius at 4.1.55-57, below. 48. **sweet wife, my dearest mother**: See commentary at 1.3.2. 49. **touch**: Like a touchstone, used to assay precious metals. Martius considers his own value by measuring the fidelity of his friends. This may explain his decision in 5.6 to call a truce with Rome. 51. **above the ground**: alive, unburied. 53. **what is like me formerly**: Martius promises not to change; to be true to his nature. In other words, in exile, he's not going to become a farmer, or suddenly love the common man. 55-57. **If I could...seven years...I'ld with thee**: If I were seven years younger, echoing Cominius' desire to accompany Martius.
SCENE II.
1. **no further**: discuss it no further. 2. **vex'd**: angered, irritated.

	Let us seem humbler after it is done
	Than when it was a-doing.

SICINUS   Bid them home.   5
Say their great enemy is gone, and they
Stand in their ancient strength.

BRUTUS   Dismiss them home.
                                          [*Exit Ædile.*]
Here comes his mother.

Enter Volumnia, Virgilia, and Menenius.

SICINUS   Let's not meet her.

BRUTUS   Why?

SICINUS   They say she's mad.

BRUTUS   They have ta'en note of us. Keep on your way.   10

VOLUMNIA   O, y'are well met. The hoarded plague o' th' gods
Requit your love!

MENENIUS   Peace, peace! Be not so loud.

VOLUMNIA   If that I could for weeping, you should hear—
Nay, and you shall hear some. [*To Brutus*]
Will you be gone?   15

VIRGILIA   [*to Sicinius*] You shall stay too. I would I had the power
To say so to my husband.

SICINUS   Are you mankind?

VOLUMNIA   Ay, fool. Is that a shame? Note but this fool!
Was not a man my father? Hadst thou foxship
To banish him that struck more blows for Rome   20
Than thou hast spoken words?

SICINUS   O blessed heavens!

VOLUMNIA   Moe noble blows than ever thou wise words,
And for Rome's good. I'll tell thee what—Yet go!
Nay, but thou shalt stay too. I would my son
Were in Arabia, and thy tribe before him,   25
His good sword in his hand.

4. **seem humbler**: The tribunes suspect they have overplayed their hand. 7. **Ancient strength**: See 3.3.17, above. 9. **mad**: insane. 10. **ta'en note of us**: noticed us. 11. **hoarded plague**: See commentary at 1.3.98. 12. **Requit your love**: revenge for your so-called love. 16. **You shall stay too**: Even the mousy Virgilia is abusive here, though she's inept. Volumnia orders them to go, she to stay. 17. **mankind**: Suggesting that Volumnia is acting unfemininely and, thus, monstrously. 19. **Was not a man my father**: Suggesting that there is some man in her. 25-26. **Arabia, and thy tribe before him,/His good sword in hand**: As the Jews were slaughtered in Medina.

SICINUS   What then?

VIRGILIA   What then?
He'ld make an end of thy posterity.

VOLUMNIA   Bastards and all.
Good man, the wounds that he does bear for Rome!

MENENIUS   Come, come, peace.

SICINUS   I would he had continued to his country   30
As he began, and not unknit himself
The noble knot he made.

BRUTUS   I would he had.

VOLUMNIA   "I would he had"? 'Twas you incens'd the rabble.
Cats, that can judge as fitly of his worth
As I can of those mysteries which heaven   35
Will not have earth to know!

BRUTUS   Pray let us go.

VOLUMNIA   Now, pray, sir, get you gone.
You have done a brave deed. Ere you go, hear this:
As far as doth the Capitol exceed
The meanest house in Rome, so far my son   40
(This lady's husband here, this! Do you see?)
Whom you have banish'd does exceed you all.

BRUTUS   Well, well, we'll leave you.

SICINUS   Why stay we to be baited
With one that wants her wits?   *Exeunt Tribunes.*

VOLUMNIA   Take my prayers with you.
I would the gods had nothing else to do   45
But to confirm my curses. Could I meet 'em
But once a day, it would unclog my heart
Of what lies heavy to't.

MENENIUS   You have told them home,
And, by my troth, you have cause. You'll sup with me?

VOLUMNIA   Anger's my meat. I sup upon myself,   50
And so shall starve with feeding.—Come, let's go

---

27. **posterity**: life. 31. **unknit**: unraveled, ruined. 33. **incens'd the rabble**: worked up the crowd to a frenzy. 34. **Cats, that can judge fitly of his worth**: It's as silly to say that you can match Martius' worth as it is to say that cats can serve as judges. 35. **mysteries which heaven**: Comparing Martius to a god. See commentary at 1.1.243. 38. **brave** deed: ironic. 43. **baited**: insulted. 44. **wants**: lacks. —**prayers**: curses. 47. **unclog**: unburdened. 48. **told them home**: spoken truth to power. 49. **sup**: dine.

Leave this faint puling, and lament as I do,
In anger, Juno-like. Come, come, come!

Exeunt [Volumnia and Virgilia].

MENENIUS   Fie, fie, fie!   *Exit.*

SCENE III. [*A highway between Rome and Antium.*]

Enter a Roman and a Volsce [meeting].

ROMAN   I know you well, sir, and you know me.
             Your name, I think, is Adrian.

VOLSCE   It is so, sir. Truly I have forgot you.

ROMAN   I am a Roman; and my services are, as you are, against 'em.
             Know you me yet?   5

VOLSCE   Nicanor? No?

ROMAN   The same, sir.

VOLSCE   You had more beard when I last saw you, but your favor is
             well approv'd by your tongue. What's the news in Rome? I
             have a note from the Volscian state to find you out there. You
             have well saved me a day's journey.   11

ROMAN   There hath been in Rome strange insurrections—the people
             against the senators, patricians, and nobles.

VOLSCE   Hath been? Is it ended then? Our state thinks not so. They
             are in a most warlike preparation and hope to come upon
             them in the heat of their division.   16

ROMAN   The main blaze of it is past, but a small thing would make it
             flame again; for the nobles receive so to heart the banishment
             of that worthy Coriolanus that they are in a ripe aptness to
             take all power from the people and to pluck from them their
             tribunes for ever. This lies glowing, I can tell you, and is
             almost mature for the violent breaking out.   22

VOLSCE   Coriolanus banish'd?

ROMAN   Banish'd, sir.

---

52. **puling**: whining, whimpering. 53. **Juno-like**: The wife of Zeus, known to take revenge against her enemies.
SCENE III
4. **Roman**: Aufidius' spy, no doubt. See 1.2.7, above. 8. **favor**: identity; Adrian recognizes his voice or his bitterness against Rome. 14. **Our state thinks not so**: So, the Volscians already knew something of the Roman uprising against Martius and the state. 16. **them**: the Romans. 17. **blaze...flame**: Incendiary imagery, see 2.1.195-99 and 4.6.137, above. 19. **ripe aptness**: ready.

| VOLSCE | You will be welcome with this intelligence, Nicanor. | 25 |

ROMAN   The day serves well for them now. I have heard it said the
fittest time to corrupt a man's wife is when she's fall'n out
with her husband. Your noble Tullus Aufidius will appear
well in these wars, his great opposer, Coriolanus, being now
in no request of his country.   30

VOLSCE   He cannot choose. I am most fortunate thus accidentally
to encounter you. You have ended my business, and I will
merrily accompany you home.

ROMAN   I shall between this and supper tell you most strange things
from Rome, all tending to the good of their adversaries. Have
you an army ready, say you?   36

VOLSCE   A most royal one,—the centurions and their charges,
distinctly billeted, already in th' entertainment and to be on
foot at an hour's warning.

ROMAN   I am joyful to hear of their readiness and am the man, I   40
think, that shall set them in present action. So, sir, heartily
well met, and most glad of your company.

VOLSCE   You take my part from me, sir. I have the most cause to be
glad of yours.

ROMAN   Well, let us go together.   *Exeunt.*   45

Scene IV. [*Antium. Before Aufidius's house.*]

Enter Martius in mean apparel, disguis'd and muffled.

MARTIUS   A goodly city is this Antium. City,
'Tis I that made thy widows. Many an heir
Of these fair edifices fore my wars

27-28. **fittest time to corrupt a man's wife is when she's fall'n out with her husband**: The wife here
is fame, who will now fall in love with Aufidius. Adding to the sexual imagery of Aufidius as a rival to
Coriolanus. See commentary at 1.1.215. 35. **adversaries**: the Volscians. 38-39. **distinctly billeted,...
at an hour's warning**: Organized and ready to march. 40-41. **am the man, I think,...present action**:
Nicanor's news will set a war in motion; it is doubtful this spy thinks he will lead the army.
Scene IV
2. **thy widows**: He killed their husbands in battle. 3. **fore my wars**: At the forehead of the battle.

Have I heard groan and drop. Then know me not,
Lest that thy wives with spits and boys with stones   5
In puny battle slay me.

Enter a Citizen.

Save you, sir.

CITIZEN   And you.

MARTIUS   Direct me, if it be your will,
Where great Aufidius lies. Is he in Antium?

CITIZEN   He is, and feasts the nobles of the state
At his house this night.

MARTIUS   Which is his house, beseech you?   10

CITIZEN   This here before you.

MARTIUS   Thank you, sir. Farewell.   *Exit Citizen.*
O world, thy slippery turns! Friends now fast sworn,
Whose double bosom seems to wear one heart,
Whose hours, whose bed, whose meal and exercise
Are still together, who twin (as 'twere) in love   15
Unseparable, shall within this hour,
On a dissension of a doit, break out
To bitterest enmity. So fellest foes,
Whose passions and whose plots have broke their sleep
To take the one the other, by some chance,   20
Some trick not worth an egg, shall grow dear friends
And interjoin their issues. So with me.
My birthplace hate I, and my love's upon
This enemy town. I'll enter. If he slay me,
He does fair justice; if he give me way,   25
I'll do his country service.   *Exit.*

6. **slay me**: Anticipating action of 5.6. 6. **Save you, sir**: A common salutation. 7. **if it be your will**: if you would be so kind. 12-21. **slippery turns**: Giddy fortune, a matter of luck, good or bad. —**Friends now fast sworn...bitterest enmity**: Good friends turned suddenly, without rhyme or reason, into sworn enemies. —**So fellest foes...friends**: If friends can become enemies, it follows that enemies can becomes friends. 22. **interjoin their issues**: Mate their love; see commentary at 1.1.215, though the point here may be that former enemies will bond their families together by intermarriage.

SCENE V. [*Antium. A hall in Aufidius's house.*]†

Music plays. Enter a Servingman.

1 SERVINGMAN   Wine, wine, wine! What service is here! I think our fellows
are asleep.   [*Exit.*]

Enter another Servingman.

2 SERVINGMAN   Where's Cotus? My master calls for him. Cotus!
                                                         Exit.

Enter Martius.

MARTIUS   A goodly house. The feast smells well, but I
Appear not like a guest.   5

Enter the first Servingman.

1 SERVINGMAN   What would you have, friend? Whence are you? Here's no
place for you. Pray go to the door.   *Exit.*

MARTIUS   I have deserv'd no better entertainment
In being Coriolanus.

Enter second Servant.

2 SERVINGMAN   Whence are you, sir? Has the porter his eyes in his head that
he gives entrance to such companions? Pray get you out.

MARTIUS   Away!

2 SERVINGMAN   Away? Get you away!

MARTIUS   Now th'art troublesome.

2 SERVINGMAN   Are you so brave? I'll have you talk'd with anon.   15

Enter third Servingman; the first meets him.

3 SERVINGMAN   What fellow's this?

1 SERVINGMAN   A strange one as ever I look'd on. I cannot get him out o' th'
house. Prithee call my master to him.

3 SERVINGMAN   What have you to do here, fellow? Pray you avoid the house.   20

SCENE V
5. **not like a guest**: uninvited. 7. **to the door**: The Servant thinks Martius is an idler looking for a
handout. 11. **to such companions**: Another indication that Martius is poorly dressed. 15. **so brave**: The
Servant is surprised by Martius' low appearance and lofty disdain.

---

†   Arrival at Antium: On Paul Scofield's *Coriolanus* (Stratford, Ontario, 1961), Walter Kerr wrote
of a "haughty man… lonely in his perpetual estrangement from his fellows. A scene in which he
arrives at the camp of his bitterest enemy… only to stand unrecognized and waiting while a couple
of clownish servants circle him … perfectly etches the helplessness of the innately proud man"
(*Hamilton Spectator*, June 30, 1961).

MARTIUS	Let me but stand. I will not hurt your hearth.
3 SERVINGMAN	What are you?
MARTIUS	A gentleman.
3 SERVINGMAN	A marv'llous poor one.
MARTIUS	True, so I am.

25

| 3 SERVINGMAN | Pray you, poor gentleman, take up some other station. Here's no place for you. Pray you avoid. Come. |
| MARTIUS | Follow your function, go and batten on cold bits. |

Pushes him away from him.

| 3 SERVINGMAN | What, you will not? Prithee tell my master what a strange guest he has here. |

30

2 SERVINGMAN	And I shall. *Exit.*
3 SERVINGMAN	Where dwell'st thou?
MARTIUS	Under the canopy.
3 SERVINGMAN	Under the canopy?
MARTIUS	Ay.

35

3 SERVINGMAN	Where's that?
MARTIUS	I' th' city of kites and crows.
3 SERVINGMAN	I' th' city of kites and crows? What an ass it is!—Then thou dwell'st with daws too?
MARTIUS	No, I serve not thy master.

40

| 3 SERVINGMAN | How, sir? Do you meddle with my master? |
| MARTIUS | Ay. 'Tis an honester service than to meddle with thy mistress. Thou prat'st and prat'st. Serve with thy trencher. Hence! |

Beats him away.

Enter Aufidius, with the [second] Servingman.

| AUFIDIUS | Where is this fellow? |

21. **hearth**: fireplace. Martius is obviously cold. 28. **function**: duties as servant. —**batten on cold bits**: gorge on leftovers. 33. **canopy**: the stars. 37. **city of kites and crows**: In the fields, where Martius won many battles, and where now the scavengers feed off the dead. 39. **daws**: jackdaws, small crows, similar to pigeons. 40. **master**: comparing Aufidius to a pigeon, pigeon-livered, cowardly, quick to take flight. 41. **meddle**: Speak of things or people who are not your concern. 43. **prat'st**: talk. —**trencher**: small plate of metal or wood.

| 2 SERVINGMAN | Here, sir. I'd have beaten him like a dog but for disturbing the lords within. | 46 |

[While Aufidius and Martius converse, the first and second Servingmen stand back.]

AUFIDIUS   Whence com'st thou? What wouldst thou? Thy name?
Why speak'st not? Speak, man. What's thy name?

MARTIUS   If, Tullus,
                                                 [Unmuffles.]
Not yet thou know'st me, and, seeing me, dost not
Think me for the man I am, necessity   50
Commands me name myself.

AUFIDIUS   What is thy name?

MARTIUS   A name unmusical to the Volscians' ears
And harsh in sound to thine.

AUFIDIUS   Say, what's thy name?
Thou hast a grim appearance, and thy face
Bears a command in't. Though thy tackle's torn,   55
Thou show'st a noble vessel. What's thy name?

MARTIUS   Prepare thy brow to frown. Know'st thou me yet?

AUFIDIUS   I know thee not. Thy name?

MARTIUS   My name is Caius Martius, who hath done
To thee particularly and to all the Volsces   60
Great hurt and mischief. Thereto witness may
My surname Coriolanus. The painful service,
The extreme dangers, and the drops of blood
Shed for my thankless country are requitted
But with that surname—a good memory   65
And witness of the malice and displeasure
Which thou shouldst bear me. Only that name remains.
The cruelty and envy of the people,
Permitted by our dastard nobles, who
Have all forsook me, hath devour'd the rest   70
And suffer'd me by th' voice of slaves to be

---

45. **I'd have beaten him like a dog**: The facts that (1) Martius is not recognized and (2) the Servant boasts of his ability to beat him suggest that Martius, while a proficient killer, is not physically formidable. 48. **Tullus**: Martius addresses him by Aufidius' first name, which suggests he still sees Aufidius as either an equal or perhaps as an inferior. Note Martius uses his full name at line 59, below. 49-50. **Not yet thou know'st me...for the man I am**: If you don't recognize me yet. 52. **unmusical**: unpleasant. 55. **tackle's torn**: Nautical image. Martius is poor, a wreck, shipwreck. 64-65. **Shed for my thankless country are requitted/But with that surname**: Suggesting that Martius expected a *quid pro quo*, reward for service. Yet this is at odds with his earlier conversation with Cominius at 1.9.18-40, above. 68. **the people**: the people of Rome. 69. **dastard nobles**: This is new. He is now expressing a rage for Menenius and Cominius as well.

Whoop'd out of Rome. Now this extremity
Hath brought me to thy hearth; not out of hope
(Mistake me not) to save my life; for if
I had fear'd death, of all the men i' th' world   75
I would have 'voided thee; but in mere spite,
To be full quit of those my banishers,
Stand I before thee here. Then if thou hast
A heart of wreak in thee, that wilt revenge
Thine own particular wrongs and stop those maims   80
Of shame seen through thy country, speed thee straight
And make my misery serve thy turn. So use it
That my revengeful services may prove
As benefits to thee; for I will fight
Against my cank'red country with the spleen   85
Of all the under fiends. But if so be
Thou dar'st not this, and that to prove more fortunes
Th'art tir'd, then, in a word, I also am
Longer to live most weary, and present
My throat to thee and to thy ancient malice;   90
Which not to cut would show thee but a fool,
Since I have ever followed thee with hate,
Drawn tuns of blood out of thy country's breast,
And cannot live but to thy shame, unless
It be to do thee service.

AUFIDIUS   O Martius, Martius!   95
Each word thou hast spoke hath weeded from my heart
A root of ancient envy. If Jupiter
Should from yond cloud speak divine things
And say "'Tis true," I'd not believe them more
Than thee, all-noble Martius. Let me twine   100
Mine arms about that body whereagainst
My grained ash an hundred times hath broke
And scarr'd the moon with splinters. Here I cleep

---

72. **Whoop'd**: cries of joy. —**extremity**: extreme situation. 73. **hearth**: home. 76. **'voided**: avoided.
79. **wreak**: vengeance. 80. **maims**: injuries, not just to soldiers but to the pride of the Volscian nation.
81. **speed thee straight**: hurry up. 82. **serve thy turn**: Use me as you wish. 85. **cank'red**: infected,
corrupted. —**spleen**: ferociousness. 86. **under fiends**: devils of Hell. 90. **My throat to thee**: Employ
me to kill Romans or kill me. —**ancient malice**: Long-standing enmity. 93. **tuns**: barrels. 96. **weeded**:
removed, playing on root in the next line. 97. **Jupiter**: King of the Roman gods; see commentary at
1.1.243. 100. **twine**: encircle. 102. **grained ash**: spear. 103. **cleep**: name, swear by.

In the 1984 BBC TV version (directed by Elijah Moshinsky), Aufidius (Mike Gwilym) passionately cupped Coriolanus' head as if to kiss him; he then began to stroke Martius' neck.

The anvil of my sword, and do contest
As hotly and as nobly with thy love   105
As ever in ambitious strength I did
Contend against thy valor. Know thou first,
I lov'd the maid I married; never man
Sigh'd truer breath. But that I see thee here,
Thou noble thing, more dances my rapt heart   110
Than when I first my wedded mistress saw
Bestride my threshold. Why, thou Mars, I tell thee
We have a power on foot, and I had purpose
Once more to hew thy target from thy brawn
Or lose mine arm for't. Thou hast beat me out   115
Twelve several times, and I have nightly since
Dreamt of encounters 'twixt thyself and me—
We have been down together in my sleep,
Unbuckling helms, fisting each other's throat—
And wak'd half dead with nothing. Worthy Martius,   120
Had we no other quarrel else to Rome but that

---

104. **anvil of my sword**: Forge, the place where Aufidius' sword was made. Perhaps a metaphor: I swear by the fire that has purified/hardened/steeled my soul, and made me the man I am. —**contest**: will strive to outdo. 110. **dances my rapt heart**: my heart skips a beat. 112. **Bestride my threshold**: In other words, entered the bridal chamber. —**Mars**: Comparing Martius to the god of war. See commentary at 1.1.243. 113. **power on foot**: An army ready to march. —**purpose**: planned. 114. **target**: shield. —**brawn**: body. 117-20. **Dreamt of encounters...half dead**: Following on from his comparison to his bride on their honeymoon, this passage reads as a wet dream. Undressing each other, shoving fists down each other's throats, i.e. oral sex, waking half dead, i.e. spent in orgasm. See commentary at 1.1.215.

Thou art thence banish'd, we would muster all
From twelve to seventy, and, pouring war
Into the bowels of ungrateful Rome,
Like a bold flood o'erbeat. O, come, go in,   125
And take our friendly senators by th' hands,
Who now are here, taking their leaves of me
Who am prepar'd against your territories,
Though not for Rome itself.

MARTIUS   You bless me, gods!

AUFIDIUS   Therefore, most absolute sir, if thou wilt have   130
The leading of thine own revenges, take
Th' one half of my commission, and set down—
As best thou art experienc'd, since thou know'st
Thy country's strength and weakness—thine own ways,
Whether to knock against the gates of Rome,   135
Or rudely visit them in parts remote
To fright them ere destroy. But come in.
Let me commend thee first to those that shall
Say yea to thy desires. A thousand welcomes!
And more a friend than e'er an enemy.   140
Yet, Martius, that was much. Your hand. Most welcome!
                        Exeunt [Martius and Aufidius].

Two of the Servingmen, [the first and second, come forward].

1 SERVINGMAN   Here's a strange alteration!

2 SERVINGMAN   By my hand, I had thought to have stroken him with a
cudgel—and yet my mind gave me his clothes made a false
report of him.   145

1 SERVINGMAN   What an arm he has! He turn'd me about with his finger and
his thumb as one would set up a top.

2 SERVINGMAN   Nay, I knew by his face that there was something in him.
He had, sir, a kind of face, methought—I cannot tell how to
term it.   150

---

122. **muster**: gather. 123. **twelve to seventy**: the age range of the soldiers. Note that at 2.2.69, above, we learn that Martius was sixteen the first time he went to war. 124. **bowels**: Stomach, ironically picking up on Menenius' imagery at 1.1.80, above. 125. **o'erbeat**: overwhelming, unstoppable. 129. **Not for Rome itself**: An essential detail, as Martius will later negotiate for Rome's surrender without actually attacking the city itself. The point is reiterated at line 135, below. 139. **yea**: agree. 141. **that was much**: Perhaps, more than you could have expected. 143-45. **stroken him with a cudgel**: Beaten him with a stick or bat. —**made a false report**: The servant assumed Martius was as humble as his clothes. 148. **something in him**: Yet no one thought him very formidable before he identified himself.

1 SERVINGMAN	He had so, looking as it were—Would I were hang'd but I thought there was more in him than I could think.
2 SERVINGMAN	So did I, I'll be sworn. He is simply the rarest man i' th' world.
1 SERVINGMAN	I think he is; but a greater soldier than he you wot on. 155
2 SERVINGMAN	Who? My master?
1 SERVINGMAN	Nay, it's no matter for that.
2 SERVINGMAN	Worth six on him.
1 SERVINGMAN	Nay, not so neither. But I take him to be the greater soldier.
2 SERVINGMAN	Faith, look you, one cannot tell how to say that. For the 160 defence of a town our general is excellent.
1 SERVINGMAN	Ay, and for an assault too.

Enter the third Servingman.

3 SERVINGMAN	O slaves, I can tell you news! news, you rascals!
BOTH 1 AND 2	What, what, what? Let's partake.
3 SERVINGMAN	I would not be a Roman, of all nations. I had as live be a 165 condemn'd man.
BOTH	Wherefore? wherefore?
3 SERVINGMAN	Why, here's he that was wont to thwack our general—Caius Martius.
1 SERVINGMAN	Why do you say "thwack our general"? 170
3 SERVINGMAN	I do not say "thwack our general," but he was always good enough for him.
2 SERVINGMAN	Come, we are fellows and friends. He was ever too hard for him. I have heard him say so himself.
1 SERVINGMAN	He was too hard for him directly, to say the troth on't. Before Corioles he scotch'd him and notch'd him like a carbonado.
2 SERVINGMAN	An he had been cannibally given, he might have broil'd and eaten him too. 178
1 SERVINGMAN	But more of thy news!

---

153. **rarest**: valuable, worthy. 155. **wot**: wait, serve. 158. **him**: Aufidius. 163. **slaves**: servants. 165. **I would not be a Roman…condemn'd**: I.e., I'd rather be a man condemned to death than face Martius in battle. 168. **thwack**: beat. 173. **too hard**: too strong. 176. **carbonado**: Meat or fish, scored and broiled. Similar to our own phrase, I'll eat his lunch.

3 SERVINGMAN	Why, he is so made on here within as if he were son and heir to Mars; set at upper end o' th' table; no question ask'd him by any of the senators but they stand bald before him. Our general himself makes a mistress of him, sanctifies himself with's hand and turns up the white o' th' eye to his discourse. But the bottom of the news is, our general is cut i' th' middle and but one half of what he was yesterday, for the other has half by the entreaty and grant of the whole table. He'll go, he says, and sole the porter of Rome gates by th' ears. He will mow all down before him and leave his passage poll'd. 189
2 SERVINGMAN	And he's as like to do't as any man I can imagine. 190
3 SERVINGMAN	Do't? He will do't; for look you, sir, he has as many friends as enemies; which friends, sir, as it were, durst not (look you, sir) show themselves (as we term it) his friends whilst he's in directitude. 195
1 SERVINGMAN	Directitude? What's that?
3 SERVINGMAN	But when they shall see, sir, his crest up again and the man in blood, they will out of their burrows, like conies after rain, and revel all with him.
1 SERVINGMAN	But when goes this forward?
3 SERVINGMAN	Tomorrow, today, presently. You shall have the drum struck up this afternoon. 'Tis as it were a parcel of their feast, and to be executed ere they wipe their lips. 202
2 SERVINGMAN	Why, then we shall have a stirring world again. This peace is nothing but to rust iron, increase tailors, and breed ballad-makers. 205
1 SERVINGMAN	Let me have war, say I. It exceeds peace as far as day does night. It's sprightly, waking, audible, and full of vent. Peace is a very apoplexy, lethargy; mull'd, deaf, sleepy, insensible; a getter of more bastard children than war's a destroyer of men.

180-81. **son and heir to Mars**: On Martius' god-like status, see commentary at 1.1.243. 182. **stand bald**: Humbly, with caps removed. 183. **mistress of him**: fawns over him. See 4.5.104-12. 188. **sole the porter of Rome gates by th'ears**: Bring Rome's gates down to the ground. 189. **poll'd**: cut, shaved, trimmed. 191. **friends**: The supposition that Martius' friends will aid him in his attack is unwarranted. It is possible that the Volscians believe that they will join Martius and the Roman patricians to put down the plebeians, but, if so, why would the Volscian servant class be in favor of that? 201. **parcel**: part-and-parcel, a foregone conclusion. 207. **vent**: wind, fart, scent. 208. **apoplexy**: weakness, paralysis.

| 2 SERVINGMAN | 'Tis so; and as war in some sort may be said to be a ravisher, so it cannot be denied but peace is a great maker of cuckolds. |

| 1 SERVINGMAN | Ay, and it makes men hate one another.   212 |

| 3 SERVINGMAN | Reason; because they then less need one another. The wars for my money! I hope to see Romans as cheap as Volscians. They are rising, they are rising. |

| BOTH 1 AND 2 | In, in, in, in!   *Exeunt.* |

SCENE VI. [*Rome. A public place.*]

Enter the two Tribunes, Sicinius and Brutus.

SICINUS   We hear not of him, neither need we fear him:
His remedies are tame. The present peace
And quietness of the people, which before
Were in wild hurry here, do make his friends
Blush that the world goes well; who rather had,   5
Though they themselves did suffer by't, behold
Dissentious numbers pest'ring streets than see
Our tradesmen singing in their shops and going
About their functions friendly.

BRUTUS   We stood to't in good time.

Enter Menenius.

Is this Menenius?   10

SICINUS   'Tis he, 'tis he! O, he is grown most kind
Of late.—Hail, sir!

MENENIUS   Hail to you both!

SICINUS   Your Coriolanus is not much miss'd
But with his friends. The commonwealth doth stand,
And so would do, were he more angry at it.   15

MENENIUS   All's well, and might have been much better if
He could have temporiz'd.

210-11. **ravisher...cuckolds**: War seduces men, just as men seduce women during peacetime. On the erotica of battle, see commentary at 1.1.215. 214. **Romans as cheap as Volscians**: the value of Roman lives, as cheap as Volscian lives.
SCENE VI.
2. **His remedies are tame**: The ways in which Martius can better himself have no effect on Rome.
4. **wild hurry**: discord, panic. 7. **Dissentious**: Quarrelsome, disaffected. 10. **stood to't**: Stood up to Martius, stood up for the people. 17. **temporiz'd**: calmed, accommodated.

SICINUS	Where is he, hear you?

MENENIUS   Nay, I hear nothing. His mother and his wife
Hear nothing from him.

Enter three or four Citizens.

ALL [CITIZENS]   The gods preserve you both!

SICINUS   Good-en, our neighbours.   20

BRUTUS   Good-en to you all, good-en to you all.

1 CITIZEN   Ourselves, our wives, and children, on our knees
Are bound to pray for you both.

SICINUS   Live and thrive!

BRUTUS   Farewell, kind neighbours. We wish'd Coriolanus
Had lov'd you as we did.

ALL [CITIZENS]   Now the gods keep you!   25

BOTH TRIBUNES   Farewell, farewell.   *Exeunt Citizens.*

SICINUS   This is a happier and more comely time
Than when these fellows ran about the streets
Crying confusion.

BRUTUS   Caius Martius was
A worthy officer i' th' war, but insolent,   30
O'ercome with pride, ambitious past all thinking,
Self-loving—

SICINUS   And affecting one sole throne
Without assistance.

MENENIUS   I think not so.

SICINUS   We should by this, to all our lamentation,
If he had gone forth consul, found it so.   35

BRUTUS   The gods have well prevented it, and Rome
Sits safe and still without him.

Enter an Ædile.

ÆDILE   Worthy tribunes,
There is a slave whom we have put in prison
Reports the Volsces with two several powers
Are ent'red in the Roman territories   40
And with the deepest malice of the war
Destroy what lies before 'em.

---

20. **Good-en**: Good evening. 29. **Crying confusion**: The irony here is that much of that confusion was engineered by the tribunes. 32. **one sole throne**: Martius wanted absolute power, the consulship. 34. **lamentation**: grief. 39. **two several powers**: two separate armies.

MENENIUS	'Tis Aufidius,
	Who, hearing of our Martius' banishment,
	Thrusts forth his horns again into the world,
	Which were inshell'd when Martius stood for Rome, 45
	And durst not once peep out.

SICINUS   Come, what talk you of Martius?

BRUTUS   Go see this rumorer whipp'd. It cannot be
The Volsces dare break with us.

MENENIUS   Cannot be?
We have record that very well it can,
And three examples of the like hath been   50
Within my age. But reason with the fellow
Before you punish him, where he heard this,
Lest you shall chance to whip your information
And beat the messenger who bids beware
Of what is to be dreaded.

SICINUS   Tell not me.   55
I know this cannot be.

BRUTUS   Not possible.

Enter a Messenger.

MESSENGER   The nobles in great earnestness are going
All to the Senate House. Some news is come
That turns their countenances.

SICINUS   'Tis this slave—
Go whip him fore the people's eyes!—his raising,   60
Nothing but his report.

MESSENGER   Yes, worthy sir.
The slave's report is seconded, and more,
More fearful, is deliver'd.

SICINUS   What more fearful?

MESSENGER   It is spoke freely out of many mouths
(How probable I do not know) that Martius,   65
Join'd with Aufidius, leads a power 'gainst Rome

44. **horns again into the world**: Horns might suggest his formidable physical nature, i.e. like a bull, or it may suggest his fearsome emotional characteristics, i.e., like a devil. However, "inshell'd" (line 45) suggests that Aufidius is being compared to a snail. If so, Menenius is reminding the tribunes that Aufidius was only harmless because Martius was around to crush him. 51. **reason**: question. 59. **turns their countenances**: turns their faces white with fear. 61. **report**: rumor.

And vows revenge as spacious as between
The young'st and oldest thing.

SICINUS   This is most likely!

BRUTUS   Rais'd only that the weaker sort may wish
Good Martius home again.

SICINUS   The very trick on't.   70

MENENIUS   This is unlikely.
He and Aufidius can no more atone
Than violent'st contrariety.

Enter [another] Messenger.

MESSENGER   You are sent for to the Senate.
A fearful army, led by Caius Martius   75
Associated with Aufidius, rages
Upon our territories, and have already
O'erborne their way, consum'd with fire and took
What lay before them.

Enter Cominius.

COMINIUS   O, you have made good work!

MENENIUS   What news? What news?   80

COMINIUS   You have holp to ravish your own daughters and
To melt the city leads upon your pates,
To see your wives dishonor'd to your noses—

MENENIUS   What's the news? What's the news?

COMINIUS   Your temples burned in their cement, and   85
Your franchises, whereon you stood, confin'd
Into an auger's bore.

MENENIUS   Pray now, your news!
You have made fair work, I fear me. Pray, your news!
If Martius should be join'd with Volscians—

67-68. **as spacious as between/The young'st and oldest**: That is, no one will be spared. 68. **This is most likely**: Disbelief—Martius would never join Aufidius. 69-70. **Rais'd only that the weaker sort may wish/Good Martius home again**: A rumor spread by the patricians/aristocrats to frighten the people into revoking Martius' banishment. 73. **violent'st contrariety**: Menenius doubts whether Martius and Aufidius could ever work together. 76. **rages**: attacks like a fever, sudden and deadly. 78. **O'erborne**: Overcome. 80. **you**: the tribunes. 81. **holp**: helped. 82. **leads**: lead roofs. **—pates**: heads. 83. **see your wives dishonor'd to your noses**: raped before your eyes. 87. **auger's bore**: A small boring tool; i.e. your rights and powers reduced to next to nothing.

COMINIUS   If? He is their god. He leads them like a thing   90
            Made by some other deity than Nature,
            That shapes man better; and they follow him
            Against us brats with no less confidence
            Than boys pursuing summer butterflies
            Or butchers killing flies.

MENENIUS   You have made good work,   95
            You and your apron-men! you that stood so much
            Upon the voice of occupation and
            The breath of garlic-eaters!

COMINIUS   He will shake
            Your Rome about your ears.

MENENIUS   As Hercules
            Did shake down mellow fruit. You have made fair work! 100

BRUTUS   But is this true, sir?

COMINIUS   Ay, and you'll look pale
            Before you find it other. All the regions
            Do smilingly revolt, and who resist
            Are mock'd for valiant ignorance
            And perish constant fools. Who is't can blame him?   105
            Your enemies and his find something in him.

MENENIUS   We are all undone unless
            The noble man have mercy.

COMINIUS   Who shall ask it?
            The tribunes cannot do't for shame. The people
            Deserve such pity of him as the wolf   110
            Does of the shepherds. For his best friends, if they
            Should say "Be good to Rome," they charg'd him even
            As those should do that had deserv'd his hate,
            And therein show'd like enemies.

90. **their god**: See commentary at 1.1.243. 93. **brats**: Roman youth, no match for the manly Martius. 94. **butterflies**: See 1.3.55-60. 96. **apron-men**: Working-class followers, ill-suited to politics, which is above their station. 98. **garlic-eaters**: See 2.1.186-96 and 2.3.52-53, above. 100. **mellow fruit**: ripe, ready to fall. One of the twelve labors of Hercules. That is, Martius will not find defeating Rome to be a great labor. 102. **other**: otherwise. 103. **smilingly revolt**: happily. 104. **valiant ignorance**: brave but stupid to resist Martius. 110-11. **wolf/Does of the shepherds**: Martius is here the shepherd who will kill the wolf. Ironic, in that the Roman people are the flock who need protection from the wolf. 112. **they charg'd him even**: Cominius argues that the patricians are partially responsible for agreeing to Martius' banishment. See 4.5.69, above.

MENENIUS	'Tis true.

If he were putting to my house the brand   115
That should consume it, I have not the face
To say "Beseech you cease." You have made fair hands,
You and your crafts! You have crafted fair!

COMINIUS   You have brought
A trembling upon Rome, such as was never
S' incapable of help.

TRIBUNES   Say not we brought it.   120

MENENIUS   How? Was it we? We lov'd him, but, like beasts
And cowardly nobles, gave way unto your clusters,
Who did hoot him out o' th' city.

COMINIUS   But I fear
They'll roar him in again. Tullus Aufidius,
The second name of men, obeys his points   125
As if he were his officer. Desperation
Is all the policy, strength, and defence
That Rome can make against them.

Enter a troop of Citizens.

MENENIUS   Here come the clusters.
And is Aufidius with him? You are they
That made the air unwholesome when you cast   130
Your stinking greasy caps in hooting at
Coriolanus' exile. Now he's coming,
And not a hair upon a soldier's head
Which will not prove a whip. As many coxcombs
As you threw caps up will he tumble down   135
And pay you for your voices. 'Tis no matter.
If he could burn us all into one coal,
We have deserv'd it.

ALL   Faith, we hear fearful news.

1 CITIZEN   For mine own part,
When I said banish him, I said 'twas pity.   140

2 CITIZEN   And so did I.

3 CITIZEN   And so did I; and, to say the truth, so did very many of us.

---

115. **brand**: torch. 118. **crafted fair**: made good work, ironic. 122. **clusters**: the mob. 124. **roar**: cries of pain. 130. **unwholesome**: On bad breath, see 2.1.186-96, 2.3.52-53, 4.6.98, above. 133-34. **hair...whip**: He'll whip you more than there are hairs on your head. 134. **coxcombs**: fools. 137. **one coal**: Reiterating the fear that Martius will burn Rome to the ground.

That we did, we did for the best; and though we willingly
consented to his banishment, yet it was against our will.

COMINIUS   Y'are goodly things, you voices!

MENENIUS   You have made   145
Good work, you and your cry! Shall's to the Capitol?

COMINIUS   O, ay! What else?   *Exeunt both.*

SICINUS   Go, masters, get you home. Be not dismay'd.
These are a side that would be glad to have
This true which they so seem to fear. Go home   150
And show no sign of fear.

1 CITIZEN   The gods be good to us! Come, masters, let's home. I ever said
we were i' th' wrong when we banish'd him.

2 CITIZEN   So did we all. But come, let's home.   *Exeunt Citizens.*

BRUTUS   I do not like this news.   155

SICINUS   Nor I.

BRUTUS   Let's to the Capitol. Would half my wealth
Would buy this for a lie!

SICINUS   Pray let us go.   *Exeunt Tribunes.*

SCENE VII. [*A camp, at a short distance from Rome.*]

Enter Aufidius with his Lieutenant.

AUFIDIUS   Do they still fly to th' Roman?

LIEUTENANT   I do not know what witchcraft 's in him, but
Your soldiers use him as the grace fore meat,
Their talk at table, and their thanks at end;
And you are dark'ned in this action, sir,   5
Even by your own.

AUFIDIUS   I cannot help it now,
Unless by using means I lame the foot
Of our design. He bears himself more proudlier,

---

146. **Shall's**: Shall we. Note that the tribunes are not invited to join them. 149. **These are a side that would be glad**: Still playing politics, the tribunes suggest that the aristocrats are happy that Martius is attacking them. 158. **buy this for a lie**: pay to find out that this, Martius' impending attack, was not so.
SCENE VII.
1. **they**: His once loyal men, who now worship Martius. 3. **grace fore meat**: prayer before eating. 5. **dark'ned**: lessened. 7. **lame**: hinder.

Even to my person, than I thought he would
When first I did embrace him. Yet his nature   10
In that's no changeling, and I must excuse
What cannot be amended.

LIEUTENANT   Yet I wish, sir
(I mean for your particular), you had not
Join'd in commission with him; but either
Had borne the action of yourself, or else   15
To him had left it solely.

AUFIDIUS   I understand thee well; and be thou sure,
When he shall come to his account, he knows not
What I can urge against him. Although it seems,
And so he thinks, and is no less apparent   20
To th' vulgar eye, that he bears all things fairly
And shows good husbandry for the Volscian state,
Fights dragon-like, and does achieve as soon
As draw his sword; yet he hath left undone
That which shall break his neck or hazard mine   25
Whene'er we come to our account.

LIEUTENANT   Sir, I beseech you, think you he'll carry Rome?

AUFIDIUS   All places yield to him ere he sits down,
And the nobility of Rome are his;
The senators and patricians love him too.   30
The tribunes are no soldiers, and their people
Will be as rash in the repeal as hasty
To expel him thence. I think he'll be to Rome
As is the osprey to the fish, who takes it
By sovereignty of nature. First he was   35
A noble servant to them, but he could not
Carry his honors even. Whether 'twas pride,
Which out of daily fortune ever taints
The happy man; whether defect of judgment,
To fail in the disposing of those chances   40
Which he was lord of; or whether nature,

---

9. **Even to my person**: Martius should hold Aufidius as an equal, but does not. 14. **Join'd in commission**: Split his command, since it seems as if Martius will get all the credit for what looks to be a sure and easy victory over Rome. 16. **solely**: soley to Martius. 17. **be thou sure**: rest assured. 18. **he shall come to his account**: I'll get even. 21. **vulgar**: common. —**fairly**: uprightly. 22. **husbandry**: care. 23. **dragon-like**: See 4.1.30, 5.4.11. 25. **hazard**: risk. 27. **carry**: defeat. 29. **the nobility of Rome are his**: See 4.5.191, above. 32. **rash**: quick. —**repeal**: This is a new idea, the expectation that Rome will come to terms with Martius before they even fight with him. 34. **osprey**: hawk that eats fish. 37-40. **even**: with equanimity, composure. —**Whether 'twas pride...fortune...whether defect of judgment,/ To fail in the disposing of those chances**: Whether by luck or accident, Martius is destined to fall. 43.

Not to be other than one thing, not moving
From th' casque to th' cushion, but commanding peace
Even with the same austerity and garb
As he controll'd the war; but one of these   45
(As he hath spices of them all, not all,
For I dare so far free him) made him fear'd,
So hated, and so banish'd. But he has a merit
To choke it in the utt'rance. So our virtues
Lie in th' interpretation of the time;   50
And power, unto itself most commendable,
Hath not a tomb so evident as a chair
T' extol what it hath done.
One fire drives out one fire; one nail, one nail;
Rights by rights falter, strengths by strengths do fail.   55
Come, let's away. When, Caius, Rome is thine,
Thou art poor'st of all; then shortly art thou mine.   *Exeunt.*

ACT V

SCENE I. [*Rome. A public place.*]

Enter Menenius, Cominius; Sicinius, Brutus, the two Tribunes; with others.

MENENIUS   No, I'll not go. You hear what he hath said
Which was sometime his general, who lov'd him
In a most dear particular. He call'd me father.
But what o' that? Go you that banish'd him;
A mile before his tent fall down, and knee   5
The way into his mercy. Nay, if he coy'd
To hear Cominius speak, I'll keep at home.

COMINIUS   He would not seem to know me.

MENENIUS   Do you hear?

COMINIUS   Yet one time he did call me by my name.

casque to th'cushion: from helmet of war to the seat of state. 44-49. **same austerity...made him fear'd.... But he has a merit/ To choke it in the utt'rance**: Merit or good qualities that silence all critiques of him, which in turn create the pent up anger that makes Martius so unpalatable to so many. 51-52. **power...tomb...chair**: The throne/chair of power will lead to his downfall/death/tomb. 55. **fail**: fall. Aufidius is plotting Martius' overthrow as soon as victory offers him the opportunity.
ACT V. SCENE I.
2. **Which was sometime his general**: Who was sometimes his general—i.e. Cominius. 5. **A mile before his tent fall down**: Recalling the Greek embassages to Achilles, who refused to fight in the Trojan War. 6. **coy'd**: refuses disdainfully.

| | I urg'd our old acquaintance, and the drops | 10 |
| | That we have bled together. Coriolanus | |

I urg'd our old acquaintance, and the drops — 10
That we have bled together. Coriolanus
He would not answer to; forbade all names.
He was a kind of nothing, titleless,
Till he had forg'd himself a name i' th' fire
Of burning Rome. — 15

MENENIUS   Why, so! You have made good work!
A pair of tribunes that have wrack'd fair Rome
To make coals cheap! A noble memory!

COMINIUS   I minded him how royal 'twas to pardon
When it was less expected. He replied, — 20
It was a bare petition of a state
To one whom they had punish'd.

MENENIUS   Very well.
Could he say less?

COMINIUS   I offered to awaken his regard
For 's private friends. His answer to me was, — 25
He could not stay to pick them in a pile
Of noisome musty chaff. He said 'twas folly,
For one poor grain or two, to leave unburnt
And still to nose th' offence.

MENENIUS   For one poor grain or two?
I am one of those! his mother, wife, his child, — 30
And this brave fellow too—we are the grains;
You are the musty chaff, and you are smelt
Above the moon. We must be burnt for you!

SICINUS   Nay, pray be patient. If you refuse your aid
In this so never-needed help, yet do not — 35
Upbraid 's with our distress. But sure, if you
Would be your country's pleader, your good tongue,
More than the instant army we can make,
Might stop our countryman.

11-15. **Coriolanus/He would not answer to...a kind of nothing...Of burning Rome**: Martius refuses all Roman honors. His new identity, however, is still connected with Rome. If he will not be Rome's protector, he will be its terror. 17. **wrack'd**: broken. 18. **coals cheap**: Turned Rome into coals to be burned into dust. Playing on "burning Rome" in 5.1.15. 19. **minded**: reminded. —**royal**: Suggesting a willingness to treat Martius as a tyrant. See 2.2.238. 21. **bare**: weak. 24. **regard**: love, affection. 26-27. **pick them in a pile/Of noisome musty chaff**: Pick a few good grains out of a rotten pile. 33. **Above the moon**: Martius, a detached being, sits, as it were, in the moon or night sky like a god. See commentary at 1.1.243. 36. **Upbraid's**: Insult us. 38-39. **More than the instant army we can make,/Might stop**: The army that might stop their Roman countryman, Martius Coriolanus. Notice that now that Martius is a threat, he's suddenly a full-fledged Roman.

MENENIUS   No, I'll not meddle.

SICINUS   Pray you go to him.

MENENIUS   What should I do?   40

BRUTUS   Only make trial what your love can do
                For Rome, towards Martius.

MENENIUS   Well, and say that Martius
                Return me, as Cominius is return'd,
                Unheard—what then?
                But as a discontented friend, grief-shot   45
                With his unkindness? Say't be so?

SICINUS   Yet your good will
                Must have that thanks from Rome after the measure
                As you intended well.

MENENIUS   I'll undertake't.
                I think he'll hear me. Yet, to bite his lip
                And hum at good Cominius much unhearts me.   50
                He was not taken well; he had not din'd.
                The veins unfill'd, our blood is cold, and then
                We pout upon the morning, are unapt
                To give or to forgive; but when we have stuff'd
                These pipes and these conveyances of our blood   55
                With wine and feeding, we have suppler souls
                Than in our priest-like fasts. Therefore I'll watch him
                Till he be dieted to my request,
                And then I'll set upon him.

BRUTUS   You know the very road into his kindness   60
                And cannot lose your way.

MENENIUS   Good faith, I'll prove him,
                Speed how it will. I shall ere long have knowledge
                Of my success.   *Exit.*

COMINIUS   He'll never hear him.

SICINUS   Not?

COMINIUS   I tell you he does sit in gold, his eye
                Red as 'twould burn Rome, and his injury   65

---

41. **make trial**: try. 43. **Return me**: I return. 47. **measure**: After you measure yourself, after you try
your best. 50. **unhearts**: disheartens. 51. **He**: Martius. 52. **blood is cold**: Harkening to the Renaissance
medical concept of the Four Humors. If the body was not in accord with itself, the personality was
distracted, not itself, echoing the tale of the belly (1.1.79-138). Ironically, had Rome released the food,
then Romans themselves would have been in a better mood and, perhaps, not have banished Martius.
58. **dieted to my request**: I'll talk to him after he's eaten and in a good mood. 59. **set upon him**: plead
to him. 61. **prove**: Try my best.

The jailer to his pity. I kneel'd before him.
'Twas very faintly he said "Rise"; dismiss'd me
Thus with his speechless hand. What he would do
He sent in writing after me, what he would not,
Bound with an oath to yield to his conditions;   70
So that all hope is vain
Unless in his noble mother and his wife,
Who, as I hear, mean to solicit him
For mercy to his country. Therefore let's hence
And with our fair entreaties haste them on.   *Exeunt.* 75

SCENE II. [*The Volscian camp before Rome.*]

Enter Menenius to the Watch on guard.

1 WATCH	Stay. Whence are you?
2 WATCH	Stand, and go back.
MENENIUS	You guard like men; 'tis well. But, by your leave,
	I am an officer of state and come
	To speak with Coriolanus.
1 WATCH	From whence?
MENENIUS	From Rome.
1 WATCH	You may not pass; you must return. Our general 5
	Will no more hear from thence.
2 WATCH	You'll see your Rome embrac'd with fire before
	You'll speak with Coriolanus.
MENENIUS	Good my friends,
	If you have heard your general talk of Rome
	And of his friends there, it is lots to blanks 10
	My name hath touch'd your ears. It is Menenius.
1 WATCH	Be it so! Go back. The virtue of your name
	Is not here passable.
MENENIUS	I tell thee, fellow,
	Thy general is my lover. I have been
	The book of his good acts, whence men have read 15

---

70. **Bound with an oath**: Sworn to serve the Volsces. A foreshadowing that Martius is not merely bound by loyalty but trapped by it. 75. **entreaties**: pleading.
SCENE II.
6. **thence**: People who come from there, Rome. 10. **lots to blanks**: like a lottery, a million-to-one. 12. **Be it so**: So be your name, but that makes no difference. 14. **my lover**: My good friend, a loved one, family. 15. **The book of his good acts**: His biggest fan.

His fame unparallel'd, haply amplified;
For I have ever verified my friends
(Of whom he's chief) with all the size that verity
Would without lapsing suffer. Nay, sometimes,
Like to a bowl upon a subtle ground,   20
I have tumbled past the throw, and in his praise
Have (almost) stamp'd the leasing. Therefore, fellow,
I must have leave to pass.

1 WATCH   Faith, sir, if you had told as many lies in his behalf as you
have uttered words in your own, you should not pass here.
No, though it were as virtuous to lie as to live chastely.
Therefore go back.   27

MENENIUS   Prithee, fellow, remember my name is Menenius, always
factionary on the party of your general.

2 WATCH   Howsoever you have been his liar, as you say you have, I am
one that, telling true under him, must say you cannot pass.
Therefore go back.   32

MENENIUS   Has he din'd, canst thou tell? For I would not speak with
him till after dinner.

1 WATCH   You are a Roman, are you?   35

MENENIUS   I am, as thy general is.

1 WATCH   Then you should hate Rome, as he does. Can you, when
you have push'd out your gates the very defender of them,
and in a violent popular ignorance given your enemy your
shield, think to front his revenges with the easy groans of
old women, the virginal palms of your daughters, or with
the palsied intercession of such a decay'd dotant as you seem
to be? Can you think to blow out the intended fire your city
is ready to flame in with such weak breath as this? No, you
are deceiv'd. Therefore, back to Rome and prepare for your
execution. You are condemn'd; our general has sworn you out
of reprieve and pardon.   47

MENENIUS   Sirrah, if thy captain knew I were here, he would use me with
estimation.

1 WATCH   Come, my captain knows you not.   50

16. **amplified**: Exaggerated. See Martius' unease throughout 1.9. 18. **with all the size that verity**: I express my true friendship by over-praising, though not over-prizing, my friends. 21. **tumbled past the throw**: Overextended myself, made myself look foolish. 26. **virtuous to lie as to live chastely**: If every lie were a blessing. 29. **factionary on**: partial to, favorable to. 33. **Has he din'd**: See 5.1.58. 40. **front**: confront, offset, turn away. 41. **virginal palms**: virgins with hands held up in supplication. 42. **dotant**: dotard, old folk. 43. **intended fire**: See 5.1.15 and 5.1.18. 46. **sworn you out of**: sworn not to listen to you. 49. **estimation**: with esteem.

MENENIUS	I mean thy general.
1 WATCH	My general cares not for you. Back, I say, go! lest I let forth your half-pint of blood. Back! That's the utmost of your having. Back!
MENENIUS	Nay, but, fellow, fellow— 55

Enter Martius with Aufidius.

MARTIUS	What's the matter?
MENENIUS	Now, you companion, I'll say an errand for you. You shall know now that I am in estimation. You shall perceive that a Jack guardant cannot office me from my son Coriolanus. Guess, but by my entertainment with him, if thou stand'st not i' th' state of hanging, or of some death more long in spectatorship and crueller in suffering. Behold now presently, and swoond for what's to come upon thee. [*To Martius*] The glorious gods sit in hourly synod about thy particular prosperity and love thee no worse than thy old father Menenius does! O my son, my son! Thou art preparing fire for us. Look thee, here's water to quench it. I was hardly moved to come to thee; but being assured none but myself could move thee, I have been blown out of our gates with sighs, and conjure thee to pardon Rome and thy petitionary countrymen. The good gods assuage thy wrath, and turn the dregs of it upon this varlet here—this, who, like a block, hath denied my access to thee. 73
MARTIUS	Away!
MENENIUS	How? Away? 75
MARTIUS	Wife, mother, child I know not. My affairs Are servanted to others. Though I owe My revenge properly, my remission lies In Volscian breasts. That we have been familiar, Ingrate forgetfulness shall poison rather 80 Than pity note how much. Therefore be gone.

52-53. **let forth your half-pint of blood**: stab, wound the little blood the old man has. 59. **Jack guardant cannot office me**: Some faceless putz cannot keep me from my old friend. 60-61. **if thou stand'st not i'th' state of hanging**: deserve hanging after the way you treated me. 63. **swoond**: faint in fear. 64. **sit in hourly synod**: meet in council hourly. 67. **water to quench it**: tears. 71. **assuage**: ease. 72. **dregs**: the small remains. **—varlet**: rascal. **—block**: fool. 77. **servanted**: sworn in service to others. 78. **remission**: pardon. 80. **Ingrate...poison**: If Martius were not to admit his debt/love to Menenius, he would be poisoned by ingratitude. As it is, he can only pity his coming doom.

Mine ears against your suits are stronger than
Your gates against my force. Yet, for I lov'd thee,
Take this along. I writ it for thy sake   [*Gives a letter.*]
And would have sent it. Another word, Menenius,   85
I will not hear thee speak. This man, Aufidius,
Was my belov'd in Rome; yet thou behold'st.

AUFIDIUS   You keep a constant temper.
                    Exeunt. Manent the Guard and Menenius.

1 WATCH   Now, sir, is your name Menenius?

2 WATCH   'Tis a spell, you see, of much power.   90
You know the way home again.

1 WATCH   Do you hear how we are shent for keeping your greatness
back?

2 WATCH   What cause do you think I have to swoond?

MENENIUS   I neither care for th' world nor your general; for such things
as you, I can scarce think there's any, y'are so slight. He that
hath a will to die by himself fears it not from another. Let
your general do his worst. For you, be that you are, long; and
your misery increase with your age! I say to you, as I was said
to, "Away!"   *Exit.* 100

1 WATCH   A noble fellow, I warrant him.

2 WATCH   The worthy fellow is our general.
He's the rock, the oak not to be wind-shaken.   *Exit Watch.*

SCENE III. [*The tent of* Coriolanus.]

Enter Martius and Aufidius, [with others].

MARTIUS   We will before the walls of Rome tomorrow
Set down our host. My partner in this action,
You must report to th' Volscian lords how plainly
I have borne this business.

AUFIDIUS   Only their ends

82-83. **your suits...Your gates**: I am better armed against you than against Rome itself. Martius has expected and prepared—steeled himself—for this encounter. 88. **constant temper**: loyal to the Volsces. 90. **spell...of much power**: ridiculing Menenius. 92. **shent**: blamed, injured. 95. **I neither care for th' world nor your general**: A sign of Menenius' bitterness. All his hope and faith is shattered. See 5.3.9. 103. **the rock**: Immoveable. Perhaps playing upon 3.1.211.
SCENE III.
1. **We will before**: We will be before. 2. **host**: army. 3. **plainly**: openly, without any regrets or sentimentality to Rome.

You have respected; stopp'd your ears against   5
The general suit of Rome; never admitted
A private whisper—no, not with such friends
That thought them sure of you.

MARTIUS   This last old man,†
Whom with a crack'd heart I have sent to Rome,
Lov'd me above the measure of a father;   10
Nay, godded me indeed. Their latest refuge
Was to send him; for whose old love I have
(Though I show'd sourly to him) once more offer'd
The first conditions, which they did refuse
And cannot now accept. To grace him only   15
That thought he could do more, a very little
I have yielded to. Fresh embassies and suits,
Nor from the state nor private friends, hereafter
Will I lend ear to. (*Shout within.*) Ha! What shout is this?
Shall I be tempted to infringe my vow   20
In the same time 'tis made? I will not.

Enter Virgilia, Volumnia, Valeria, Young Martius, with Attendants.

My wife comes foremost; then the honor'd mould
Wherein this trunk was fram'd, and in her hand
The grandchild to her blood. But out, affection!
All bond and privilege of nature, break!   25
Let it be virtuous to be obstinate.
What is that curtsy worth? or those dove's eyes,
Which can make gods forsworn? I melt and am not
Of stronger earth than others. My mother bows,
As if Olympus to a molehill should   30
In supplication nod; and my young boy
Hath an aspect of intercession which
Great Nature cries "Deny not."—Let the Volsces
Plough Rome and harrow Italy! I'll never
Be such a gosling to obey instinct, but stand   35

6. **suit**: pleas. 11. **refuge**: hope. 14. **first conditions**: The letter he gave Menenius at 5.2.84. Since Rome refuses it, it must entail their absolute surrender. 19. **lend ear to**: listen to. 20. **infringe my vow**: bend, break my oath. 22. **mould**: Martius must think he looks like his mother. See my introduction, in which I argue that Martius' manly virtues were instilled by his mother. 26. **obstinate**: stubborn. 27. **dove's eyes**: His wife's eyes, presumably. 28-29. **I...am not/ Of stronger earth than others**: This is the first time Martius has admitted he is not a god or at least godlike. 30. **Olympus to a molehill**: In other words, as if a giant should bow to an ant. 32. **intercession**: plead, prayer. 34. **Plough Rome**: Turn Rome into empty fields, as Rome did with Carthage in 146BC. 35. **gosling**: young goose, unsteady.

† Giving in to his family: Nicol Williamson's Coriolanus "gives a heart-searching impression of a man being torn apart by conflicting loyalties" (RSC, Aldwych Theatre, 1973; dir. Trevor Nunn, as discussed in Milton Shulman, *Evening Standard*, October 23, 1973).

As if a man were author of himself
And knew no other kin.

VIRGILIA   My lord and husband!

MARTIUS   These eyes are not the same I wore in Rome.

VIRGILIA   The sorrow that delivers us thus chang'd
Makes you think so.

MARTIUS   Like a dull actor now,   40
I have forgot my part and I am out,
Even to a full disgrace. Best of my flesh,
Forgive my tyranny; but do not say
For that, "Forgive our Romans." O, a kiss
Long as my exile, sweet as my revenge!   45
Now by the jealous queen of heaven, that kiss
I carried from thee, dear, and my true lip
Hath virgin'd it e'er since. You gods! I prate
And the most noble mother of the world
Leave unsaluted. Sink, my knee, i' th' earth;   *Kneels.* 50
Of thy deep duty more impression show
Than that of common sons.

VOLUMNIA   O, stand up bless'd! [*Raises him.*]
Whilst with no softer cushion than the flint
I kneel before thee, and unproperly
Show duty, as mistaken all this while   55
Between the child and parent.   [*Kneels; he raises her.*]

MARTIUS   What is this?
Your knees to me? To your corrected son?
Then let the pebbles on the hungry beach
Fillop the stars! Then let the mutinous winds
Strike the proud cedars 'gainst the fiery sun,   60
Murd'ring impossibility, to make
What cannot be, slight work!

---

36. **As if a man were author of himself**: This is delusion on Martius' part. See the Introduction, in which I argue that Martius' identity remains tied to Rome. 41. **out**: Forgot my lines. 42. **Best of my flesh**: He may be talking to himself, addressing his iron will, as he does, on line 50, his knee. 43. **tyranny**: My unwillingness to hear your pleas. 46. **jealous queen of heaven**: Juno; see 2.1.88 for her connection to Rome. 48. **Hath virgin'd it**: Martius has not strayed sexually. —**prate**: babble. 51. **thy**: his knee. 53. **flint**: the hard stone. 54-55. **unproperly...mistaken**: A son should show devotion to the mother, thus mistaken. Volumnia here admits that her son's behavior is her fault and begs his forgiveness. 57. **corrected**: Shamed, because his mother kneels to him. 58. **hungry**: Perhaps barren, sterile, thus weak. Alternatively, Martius may have in mind the ships lost at sea by the hungry and devouring waves. 59. **Fillop**: knock, smash. 61. **Murd'ring impossibility**: Making the impossible possible.

Coriolanus (Alan Howard) embraces and, ultimately, succumbs to his mother (Irene Worth) (Coriolanus, BBC 1984).

VOLUMNIA	Thou art my warrior; I holp to frame thee. Do you know this lady?
MARTIUS	The noble sister of Publicola, The moon of Rome, chaste as the icicle 65 That's curded by the frost from purest snow And hangs on Dian's temple! Dear Valeria!
VOLUMNIA	This is a poor epitome of yours, Which by th' interpretation of full time May show like all yourself.
MARTIUS	The god of soldiers, 70 With the consent of supreme Jove, inform Thy thoughts with nobleness, that thou mayst prove To shame unvulnerable, and stick i' th' wars Like a great seamark, standing every flaw And saving those that eye thee!
VOLUMNIA	Your knee, sirrah. 75
MARTIUS	That's my brave boy!
VOLUMNIA	Even he, your wife, this lady, and myself Are suitors to you.

---

63. **holp**: helped. 63. **this lady**: Valeria. 64. **Publicola**: Playing on Valeria's name with Publius Valerius Publicola, one of Rome's first consuls, after the expulsion of Tarquin. See 2.1.131 and 2.2.84. 68-70. **This is a poor epitome of yours...like all yourself**: Martius' son. 70-75. **The god of soldiers... unvulnerable...eye thee**: Martius here blesses his son with the hope that he will be a great warrior like Achilles, who was dipped in the River Styx and made invulnerable to human weaponry. —**Your knee, sirrah**: Volumnia orders her grandson to kneel. He refuses, which pleases Martius.

MARTIUS
                          I beseech you, peace!
Or, if you'ld ask, remember this before:
The thing I have forsworn to grant may never   80
Be held by you denials. Do not bid me
Dismiss my soldiers or capitulate
Again with Rome's mechanics. Tell me not
Wherein I seem unnatural. Desire not
T' allay my rages and revenges with   85
Your colder reasons.

VOLUMNIA
                          O, no more, no more!
You have said you will not grant us anything;
For we have nothing else to ask but that
Which you deny already: yet we will ask,
That, if you fail in our request, the blame   90
May hang upon your hardness. Therefore hear us.

MARTIUS
Aufidius, and you Volsces, mark; for we'll
Hear naught from Rome in private.—Your request?

VOLUMNIA
Should we be silent and not speak, our raiment
And state of bodies would bewray what life   95
We have led since thy exile. Think with thyself
How more unfortunate than all living women
Are we come hither; since that thy sight, which should
Make our eyes flow with joy, hearts dance with comforts,
Constrains them weep and shake with fear and sorrow, 100
Making the mother, wife, and child to see
The son, the husband, and the father tearing
His country's bowels out. And to poor we
Thine enmity's most capital. Thou barr'st us
Our prayers to the gods, which is a comfort   105
That all but we enjoy. For how can we,
Alas, how can we for our country pray,
Whereto we are bound, together with thy victory,
Whereto we are bound? Alack, or we must lose
The country, our dear nurse, or else thy person,   110
Our comfort in the country. We must find
An evident calamity, though we had

---

81. **held**: gained. 83. **mechanics**: working class. 85. **allay**: Set aside. 91. **hardness**: obstinacy. 93. **in private**: privately. 94. **raiment**: clothing. Perhaps Volumnia and the others have come in supplicatory robes, echoing Martius's own gown of humility. See 2.3.32 sd. 95. **bewray**: explain, expose. 101. **mother, wife, and child**: Volumnia's insistence that she is a weak woman contradicts her more masculine assertions at 1..3.27, 1.3.54, 3.2.24. 103. **country's bowels**: Evoking the body politic, which Martius is now mutilating. See 1.1.79. 112. **evident calamity**: Disaster in either instance; either Rome is destroyed or Martius is captured and lead through the streets of Rome in chains (see text at 5.3.115).

Our wish, which side should win; for either thou
Must as a foreign recreant be led
With manacles thorough our streets, or else   115
Triumphantly tread on thy country's ruin
And bear the palm for having bravely shed
Thy wife and children's blood. For myself, son,
I purpose not to wait on fortune till
These wars determine. If I cannot persuade thee   120
Rather to show a noble grace to both parts
Than seek the end of one, thou shalt no sooner
March to assault thy country than to tread
(Trust to't, thou shalt not) on thy mother's womb
That brought thee to this world.

VIRGILIA   Ay, and on mine,   125
That brought you forth this boy to keep your name
Living to time.

BOY   'A shall not tread on me!
I'll run away till I am bigger, but then I'll fight.

MARTIUS   Not of a woman's tenderness to be
Requires nor child nor woman's face to see.   130
I have sat too long.   [Rises.]

VOLUMNIA   Nay, go not from us thus!
If it were so that our request did tend
To save the Romans, thereby to destroy
The Volsces whom you serve, you might condemn us
As poisonous of your honor. No! our suit   135
Is that you reconcile them while the Volsces
May say "This mercy we have show'd," the Romans,
"This we receiv'd," and each in either side
Give the all-hail to thee and cry "Be blest
For making up this peace!" Thou know'st, great son,   140
The end of war's uncertain, but this certain,
That, if thou conquer Rome, the benefit
Which thou shalt thereby reap is such a name
Whose repetition will be dogg'd with curses,
Whose chronicle thus writ, "The man was noble,   145
But with his last attempt he wip'd it out,

---

114. **recreant**: faithless, traitorous. 117. **bear the palm**: Victory wreath. See 1.3.13. 123-24. **tread/...on thy mother's womb**: Volumnia promises to commit suicide if Martius attacks Rome. 127. **'A**: They, the Volsces. 135. **poisonous**: lethal. 135-40. **No...peace**: Volumnia's suggestion, that Martius broker an honorable peace, demonstrates she has a sense of *Realpolitick*. Note that it was she who wanted her son to become consul and advised that he placate the plebeians. 141. **war's uncertain**: While this is true, it is unlikely to convince Martius, who has never lost a battle.

Destroy'd his country, and his name remains
To th' ensuing age abhorr'd." Speak to me, son.
Thou hast affected the fine strains of honor,
To imitate the graces of the gods,   150
To tear with thunder the wide cheeks o' th' air,
And yet to charge thy sulphur with a bolt
That should but rive an oak. Why dost not speak?
Think'st thou it honorable for a noble man
Still to remember wrongs? Daughter, speak you.   155
He cares not for your weeping. Speak thou, boy.
Perhaps thy childishness will move him more
Than can our reasons. There's no man in the world
More bound to's mother; yet here he lets me prate
Like one i' th' stocks. Thou hast never in thy life   160
Show'd thy dear mother any courtesy,
When she (poor hen), fond of no second brood,
Has cluck'd thee to the wars, and safely home
Loaden with honor. Say my request's unjust,
And spurn me back. But if it be not so,   165
Thou art not honest, and the gods will plague thee
That thou restrain'st from me the duty which
To a mother's part belongs. He turns away.
Down, ladies! Let us shame him with our knees.
To his surname Coriolanus 'longs more pride   170
Than pity to our prayers. Down! And end!   [*They kneel.*]
This is the last. So, we will home to Rome
And die among our neighbours. Nay, behold 's!
This boy, that cannot tell what he would have
But kneels and holds up hands for fellowship,   175
Does reason our petition with more strength
Than thou hast to deny't. Come, let us go.   [*They rise.*]
This fellow had a Volscian to his mother;
His wife is in Corioles, and this child

---

148. **ensuing age**: an appeal to posterity. Oddly, she suggests that, although Martius does not care about what people think of him now, he will care about what future generations think of him. 150-53. **the gods/…an oak**: A difficult passage. In essence, the gods have great power but rarely aim it at men. If you are going to imitate the gods, imitate their forbearance as well. 158-59: **There's no man in the world/More bound to's mother**: See Introduction on their relationship. —**prate**: babble, talk. 160-61. **stocks**: A form of punishment and public shaming. —**Thou hast never in thy life/Show'd thy dear mother any courtesy**: Contradicting her statement at 158-59. 162. **second brood**: second child. 163. **cluck'd thee to the wars**: Sending her son to war hardly demonstrates the maternal sensibilities of a mother hen! 166. **plague thee**: Presumably, for ingratitude. 175. **fellowship**: solidarity, and asking, presumably, for Martius to join them again as one family. 178. **Volscian to his mother**: Again trying to instill guilt in her son.

Like him by chance. Yet give us our dispatch.   180
I am hush'd until our city be afire.
And then I'll speak a little.

He holds her by the hand, silent.

MARTIUS   O mother, mother!†
What have you done? Behold, the heavens do ope,
The gods look down, and this unnatural scene
They laugh at. O my mother, mother! O!   185
You have won a happy victory to Rome;
But for your son—believe it, O believe it!—
Most dangerously you have with him prevail'd,
If not most mortal to him.† But let it come.
Aufidius, though I cannot make true wars,   190
I'll frame convenient peace. Now, good Aufidius,
Were you in my stead, would you have heard
A mother less? or granted less, Aufidius?

AUFIDIUS   I was mov'd withal.

MARTIUS   I dare be sworn you were!
And, sir, it is no little thing to make   195
Mine eyes to sweat compassion. But, good sir,
What peace you'll make, advise me. For my part,
I'll not to Rome, I'll back with you; and pray you
Stand to me in this cause. O mother! wife!

AUFIDIUS   [*aside*] I am glad thou hast set thy mercy and thy honor   200
At difference in thee. Out of that I'll work
Myself a former fortune.

MARTIUS   Ay, by-and-by.

---

180. **dispatch**: Permission to go, again reversing the normal course of things. A child should ask a parent for permission to leave. Note that in these reversals, Volumnia is treating Martius like a child. 182.sd. **He**: Martius. 184. **unnatural scene**: Unnatural in that the family has been split, the mother kneels to the child, etc. 185. **They laugh at**: Note that Martius sees himself as a mortal, not a god. See commentary at 1.1.243. 187-89. **But for your son...most mortal to him**: Martius understands that his betrayal will result in his death. 191. **convenient**: Easy terms for both parties, though what and why either side will concede is unclear. 196. **sweat compassion**: Martius or Auldifius might have been crying. 198. **I'll not to Rome**: Not return to Rome. 199. **to me**: with me. —**O mother! Wife!**: See 1.3.2. 200. **mercy and thy honor**: mercy for Rome and personal honor. 202. **Myself a former fortune**: Regain my former glory as a greatest warrior of the Volscians. —**Ay, by-and-by**: Martius might here be reacting to a silent plea by his family that he go with them. It is odd that there is no stage direction for a family hug. There is, then, no real good-bye, though there may be an acknowledgement that Martius is already doomed to death.

---

† A death sentence: Coriolanus (Steven Marzolf) hands his gun to his mother, symbolizing his emasculation and certain death. On Volumnia's (Celeste Ciulla) reentry to Rome, she seems lost amidst the fanfare (Olde Globe, San Diego, 2009; dir. Darko Tresnjak).

But we will drink together; and you shall bear
A better witness back than words, which we,
On like conditions, will have counterseal'd.   205
Come, enter with us. Ladies, you deserve
To have a temple built you. All the swords
In Italy, and her confederate arms,
Could not have made this peace.   *Exeunt.*

SCENE IV. [*Rome. A public place.*]

Enter Menenius and Sicinius.

MENENIUS   See you yond coign o' th' Capitol, yond cornerstone?

SICINIUS   Why, what of that?

MENENIUS   If it be possible for you to displace it with your little finger,
there is some hope the ladies of Rome, especially his mother,
may prevail with him. But I say there is no hope in't. Our   5
throats are sentenc'd and stay upon execution.

SICINIUS   Is't possible that so short a time can alter the condition of a
man?

MENENIUS   There is difference between a grub and a butterfly; yet your
butterfly was a grub. This Martius is grown from man to   10
dragon. He has wings; he's more than a creeping thing.

SICINIUS   He lov'd his mother dearly.

MENENIUS   So did he me; and he no more remembers his mother now
than an eight-year-old horse. The tartness of his face sours
ripe grapes. When he walks, he moves like an engine, and   15
the ground shrinks before his treading. He is able to pierce
a corslet with his eye, talks like a knell, and his hum is a
battery. He sits in his state, as a thing made for Alexander.
What he bids be done is finish'd with his bidding. He wants

---

204. **better witness back than words**: Possibly, a written offer, though more likely the fact that the
embassaries return alive and joyous. Note that Martius thinks that he has made his family happy, and
is ready to die in the belief. Perhaps a response to 5.3.158-59.
SCENE IV.
1. **coign**: foundation stone. 6. **throats are sentenc'd**: Sentenced to be executed. Menenius may further
rebuke the tribune Sicinius Velutus here for his words, which roused the people against Martius. 7-8.
alter the condition of a man: Perhaps the strongest indication that Sicinius Velutus understands that
the charges against Martius were not in Rome's best interest. 9. **butterfly**: echoing 1.3.57-58. 11. **dragon**:
echoing 4.1.30 and 4.7.23. 14. **an eight-year-old horse**: echoing 1.4.5, 1.9.60. —**tartness**: bitterness,
perhaps recalling 5.1.59. 17. **corslet**: light armor. —**talks like a knell**: a ring of doom, remorseless. 18.
Alexander: Alexander the Great, who ruled all of Greece and much of Asia, worshipped as a god in
Egypt when he conquered that country in 332–331 BC.

	nothing of a god but eternity and a heaven to throne in. 20
SICINIUS	Yes, mercy, if you report him truly.
MENENIUS	I paint him in the character. Mark what mercy his mother shall bring from him. There is no more mercy in him than there is milk in a male tiger. That shall our poor city find; and all this is long of you. 25
SICINIUS	The gods be good unto us!
MENENIUS	No, in such a case the gods will not be good unto us. When we banish'd him, we respected not them; and, he returning to break our necks, they respect not us.

Enter a Messenger.

MESSENGER	Sir, if you'ld save your life, fly to your house. 30
	The plebeians have got your fellow tribune†
	And hale him up and down; all swearing, if
	The Roman ladies bring not comfort home,
	They'll give him death by inches.

Enter another Messenger.

SICINIUS	What's the news?
MESSENGER	Good news, good news! The ladies have prevail'd, 35
	The Volscians are dislodg'd, and Martius gone.
	A merrier day did never yet greet Rome;
	No, not th' expulsion of the Tarquins.
SICINIUS	Friend,
	Art thou certain this is true? Is it most certain?
MESSENGER	As certain as I know the sun is fire. 40
	Where have you lurk'd that you make doubt of it?
	Ne'er through an arch so hurried the blown tide
	As the recomforted through th' gates. Why, hark you!
	Trumpets, hautboys; drums beat; all together.

---

25. **long of you**: All the blame belongs to you. 27-28. **the gods will not be good unto us. When we banish'd him, we respected them not**: Menenius here suggests that the Romans have broken a sacred covenant with the gods of Rome. 31. **fellow tribune**: Brutus or, as he is called in the *Dramatis Personæ*, Junius Brutus. 34. **death by inches**: Every inch of him will be tortured and executed. 36. **The Volscians are dislodg'd**: The army has moved off. The threat to Rome is over. 38. **Tarquins**: Ironically, Martius was instrumental in their overthrow. See 2.1.131, 2.2.84, above. 42-43. **Ne'er through an arch...th' gates**: Wind does not move as quickly as this good news.

---

† On news that the people have turned against the tribunes: James Newcomb and Grant Goodman, playing the role of the tribunes, rush off stage. Two single shots are heard (Olde Globe, San Diego, 2009; dir. Darko Tresnjak).

The trumpets, sackbuts, psalteries, and fifes,
Tabors and cymbals and the shouting Romans   45
Make the sun dance. Hark you!   *A shout within.*

MENENIUS   This is good news.
I will go meet the ladies. This Volumnia
Is worth of consuls, senators, patricians,
A city full; of tribunes such as you,
A sea and land full. You have pray'd well today.   50
This morning for ten thousand of your throats
I'd not have given a doit. Hark, how they joy!
                              Sound still with the shouts.

SICINIUS   First, the gods bless you for your tidings; next,
Accept my thankfulness.

MESSENGER   Sir, we have all
Great cause to give great thanks.

SICINIUS   They are near the city.   55

MESSENGER   Almost at point to enter.

SICINIUS   We will meet them
And help the joy.
                                        Exeunt.

SCENE V. [*Rome. A street near the gate.*]

*Enter two Senators, with Ladies, [Volumnia, Virgilia, Valeria,]
passing over the stage, with other Lords.*

SENATOR   Behold our patroness, the life of Rome!
Call all your tribes together, praise the gods,
And make triumphant fires; strew flowers before them.
Unshout the noise that banish'd Martius;
Repeal him with the welcome of his mother.   5
Cry, "Welcome, ladies, welcome!"

ALL   Welcome, ladies, Welcome!
                    A flourish with drums and trumpets. [*Exeunt.*]

44-45. **sackbuts, psalteries, and fifes,/ Tabors and cymbals**: Music in the streets; presumably, people are dancing and celebrating. 48. **Is worth of**: Is worth more than. 52. **doit**: a penny.
SCENE V.
1. **patroness**: Volumnia. 4. **Unshout the noise that banish'd Martius**: Volumnia's triumph rings of the odd relationship she has had with her son, who fought not just for Rome but also, perhaps even primarily, for his mother's approval. See Volumnia's fantasy of being a warrior at 1.3.26-34.

SCENE VI. [*Corioles. A public place.*]

Enter Tullus Aufidius, with Attendants.

AUFIDIUS   Go tell the lords o' th' city I am here.
Deliver them this paper. Having read it,
Bid them repair to th' market place, where I,
Even in theirs and in the commons' ears,
Will vouch the truth of it. Him I accuse   5
The city ports by this hath enter'd and
Intends t' appear before the people, hoping
To purge himself with words. Dispatch. [*Exeunt Attendants.*]

Enter three or four Conspirators of Aufidius' faction.

Most welcome!

1 CONSPIRATOR   How is it with our general?

AUFIDIUS   Even so
As with a man by his own alms empoison'd   10
And with his charity slain.

2 CONSPIRATOR   Most noble sir,
If you do hold the same intent wherein
You wish'd us parties, we'll deliver you
Of your great danger.

AUFIDIUS   Sir, I cannot tell.
We must proceed as we do find the people.   15

3 CONSPIRATOR   The people will remain uncertain whilst
'Twixt you there's difference; but the fall of either
Makes the survivor heir of all.

AUFIDIUS   I know it;
And my pretext to strike at him admits
A good construction. I rais'd him, and I pawn'd   20
Mine honor for his truth; who being so heighten'd,
He watered his new plants with dews of flattery,
Seducing so my friends; and to this end

SCENE VI.
2. **paper**: Presumably, an account of Martius' traitorous peace accord with the Romans. 3. **repair**: meet.
5. **Him**: Martius. 8. **purge**: As in the poison mentioned on line 10. 11. **charity**: Aufidius did allow
Martius to lead the army against Rome; see 5.6.30-40. 13. **wish'd us parties**: A conspiracy is in the
works, though Martius must have supporters or the exchange would not be as secretive and oblique as it
is. 19. **pretext**: rationale. 20. **pawn'd**: Vouched for him. 22. **his new plants**: His fresh seeds/seedlings,
watered and grown with the false promise of a wonderful garden, crop/harvest/victory over Rome.

	He bow'd his nature, never known before	
	But to be rough, unswayable, and free.	25
3 CONSPIRATOR	Sir, his stoutness	
	When he did stand for consul, which he lost	
	By lack of stooping—	
AUFIDIUS	That I would have spoke of.	

AUFIDIUS   That I would have spoke of.
Being banish'd for't, he came unto my hearth,
Presented to my knife his throat. I took him;   30
Made him joint-servant with me; gave him way
In all his own desires; nay, let him choose
Out of my files, his projects to accomplish,
My best and freshest men; serv'd his designments
In mine own person; holp to reap the fame   35
Which he did end all his, and took some pride
To do myself this wrong; till at the last
I seem'd his follower, not partner, and
He wag'd me with his countenance as if
I had been mercenary.

1 CONSPIRATOR   So he did, my lord.   40
The army marvell'd at it; and, in the last,
When he had carried Rome and that we look'd
For no less spoil than glory—

AUFIDIUS   There was it!
For which my sinews shall be stretch'd upon him.
At a few drops of women's rheum, which are   45
As cheap as lies, he sold the blood and labor
Of our great action. Therefore shall he die,
And I'll renew me in his fall. But hark!

Drums and trumpets sound, with great shouts of the people.

1 CONSPIRATOR   Your native town you enter'd like a post
And had no welcomes home; but he returns   50
Splitting the air with noise.

24-27. **bow'd his nature…By lack of stooping**: This is new. That Martius, while unbending and aloof with the Romans, was charming and dissembling with the Volscians. 31. **joint-servant**: Co-leaders. 33. **files**: officers and soldiers. —**projects**: His battle plans. 34. **designments**: designs, preparations. 35. **holp to reap**: helped to gain. 36. **end all his**: which seemed the end/aim of his preparations. 39. **wag'd me**: measured my worth dismissively. 43. **spoil**: spoils of war, loot. 44. **stretch'd upon him**: strained in action against him. 45. **rheum**: tears. 49. **post**: dumb, silent. 51. **Splitting the air with noise**: Echoing Volumnia's triumphant return to Rome.

2 CONSPIRATOR	And patient fools,
	Whose children he hath slain, their base throats tear
	With giving him glory.
3 CONSPIRATOR	Therefore, at your vantage,
	Ere he express himself or move the people
	With what he would say, let him feel your sword, 55
	Which we will second. When he lies along,
	After your way his tale pronounc'd shall bury
	His reasons with his body.
AUFIDIUS	Say no more.
	Here come the lords.

Enter the Lords of the city.

ALL LORDS	You are most welcome home.
AUFIDIUS	I have not deserv'd it. 60
	But, worthy lords, have you with heed perus'd
	What I have written to you?
ALL	We have.
1 LORD	And grieve to hear't.
	What faults he made before the last, I think
	Might have found easy fines; but there to end
	Where he was to begin, and give away 65
	The benefit of our levies, answering us
	With our own charge, making a treaty where
	There was a yielding—this admits no excuse.
AUFIDIUS	He approaches. You shall hear him.

Enter Martius, marching with Drum and Colors, the Commoners being with him.

MARTIUS	Hail, lords! I am return'd your soldier; 70
	No more infected with my country's love
	Than when I parted hence, but still subsisting
	Under your great command. You are to know
	That prosperously I have attempted, and
	With bloody passage led your wars even to 75
	The gates of Rome. Our spoils we have brought home
	Doth more than counterpoise a full third part

53. **at your vantage**: to your advantage. 54. **Ere he express himself**: Again, the suggestion is that Martius really has found a home among the Volscians. See 5.6.21-22, above. 61. **heed perus'd**: read with attention. 63. **the last**: the last action, Martius' surrender to or appeasement of Rome. 64. **easy fines**: lightly blamed. 66. **levies**: army positions. 68. **yielding**: retreat. 71. **infected**: See commentary at 1.3.98. 72. **subsisting**: meekly serving. 77. **a full third part**: On investment, the Volsces are up 33% on war loot.

The charges of the action. We have made peace
With no less honor to the Antiates
Than shame to th' Romans; and we here deliver,   80
Subscrib'd by th' consuls and patricians,
Together with the seal o' th' Senate, what
We have compounded on.

AUFIDIUS   Read it not, noble lords;
But tell the traitor in the highest degree
He hath abus'd your powers.   85

MARTIUS   Traitor? How now?

AUFIDIUS   Ay, traitor, Martius.

MARTIUS   Martius?

AUFIDIUS   Ay, Martius, Caius Martius! Dost thou think
I'll grace thee with that robbery, thy stol'n name
Coriolanus, in Corioles?
You lords and heads o' th' state, perfidiously   90
He has betray'd your business and given up,
For certain drops of salt, your city Rome
(I say "your city") to his wife and mother;
Breaking his oath and resolution like
A twist of rotten silk; never admitting   95
Counsel o' th' war; but at his nurse's tears
He whin'd and roar'd away your victory,
That pages blush'd at him, and men of heart
Look'd wond'ring each at other.

MARTIUS   Hear'st thou, Mars?

AUFIDIUS   Name not the god, thou boy of tears!

MARTIUS   Ha!   100

AUFIDIUS   No more.

MARTIUS   Measureless liar, thou hast made my heart
Too great for what contains it. Boy? O slave!†

---

79. **Antiates**: People of Antium, the Volsces. 83. **compounded**: agreed. 88. **stol'n name**: worthy of the man who once conquered Corioli. 90. **perfidiously**: treacherously. 91. **business**: interests. 92. **drops of salt**: tears. 95. **twist of rotten silk**: easily torn. 96. **nurse's**: mother's. 98. **pages**: young serving-boys. 99. **Mars**: God of War, reminding Aufidius of his own language at 4.5.112. 100. **boy of tears**: cry baby.

---

† Goading the Volscians to finish him off: Alan Howard (RSC, 1977; dir. Terry Hands) voiced a strong inward-breathing gasp. The soldiers took a defensive stance. Howard's next two words were unleashed furiously—'*Mea…sure… less… LIAR!*' His passion rose as he repeated "Boy!" and he taunted the surrounding soldiers: "Cut me to pieces…." (David Daniell, '*Coriolanus' in Europe*, London: Athlone Press, 40-41, 166).

Berkoff's Coriolanus is executed by Aufidius, though in Shakespeare's version it is the Conspirators who do the deed (*Coriolanus*, Globe Theatre, Tokyo, 1997).

	Pardon me, lords; 'tis the first time that ever	
	I was forc'd to scold. Your judgments, my grave lords,	105
	Must give this cur the lie; and his own notion—	
	Who wears my stripes impress'd upon him, that	
	Must bear my beating to his grave—shall join	
	To thrust the lie unto him.	
1 LORD	Peace both, and hear me speak.	110
MARTIUS	Cut me to pieces, Volsces. Men and lads,	
	Stain all your edges on me. Boy? False hound!	
	If you have writ your annals true, 'tis there,	
	That, like an eagle in a dovecote, I	
	Flutter'd your Volscians in Corioles.	115
	Alone I did it. Boy?	
AUFIDIUS	Why, noble lords,	
	Will you be put in mind of his blind fortune,	
	Which was your shame, by this unholy braggart?	
	Fore your own eyes and ears?	
ALL CONSPIRATORS	Let him die for't!	
ALL PEOPLE	Tear him to pieces!—Do it presently!—	120
	He kill'd my son!—My daughter!—He kill'd my	
	Cousin Marcus!—He kill'd my father!	

104-05. **the first time that ever/I was forc'd to scold**: He must mean since joining the Volsces. 106. **cur**: dog. 107. **stripes**: scars, Martius has beat him repeatedly in battle. 109. **thrust**: threatening a sword thrust. 112. **False hound**: leading the people on the wrong trail. 115. **flutter'd**: scattered. 116. **Alone I did it**: Goading Audifius to react. 117. **blind fortune**: good luck, unmerited.

2 LORD   Peace, ho! No outrage! Peace!
                         The man is noble, and his fame folds in
                         This orb o' th' earth. His last offences to us   125
                         Shall have judicious hearing. Stand, Aufidius,
                         And trouble not the peace.

MARTIUS   O that I had him,
                         With six Aufidiuses, or more—his tribe,
                         To use my lawful sword!

AUFIDIUS   Insolent villain!

ALL CONSPIRATORS Kill, kill, kill, kill, kill him!

        Draw the Conspirators, and kill Martius, who falls. Aufidius stands on him.

LORDS   Hold, hold, hold, hold!   130

AUFIDIUS   My noble masters, hear me speak.

1 LORD   O Tullus!

2 LORD   Thou hast done a deed whereat valor will weep.

3 LORD   Tread not upon him. Masters all, be quiet!
                         Put up your swords.

AUFIDIUS   My lords, when you shall know (as in this rage   135
                         Provok'd by him you cannot) the great danger
                         Which this man's life did owe you, you'll rejoice
                         That he is thus cut off. Please it your Honors
                         To call me to your Senate, I'll deliver
                         Myself your loyal servant or endure   140
                         Your heaviest censure.

1 LORD   Bear from hence his body,
                         And mourn you for him. Let him be regarded
                         As the most noble corse that ever herald
                         Did follow to his urn.

2 LORD   His own impatience
                         Takes from Aufidius a great part of blame.   145
                         Let's make the best of it.

---

124. **fame folds**: Difficult. Perhaps, his fame is rooted in the earth, a natural monument of greatness.
126. **judicious hearing**: echoing the show trial of Martius in 3.3. 130. **Hold**: Stop. 132. **whereat**: upon
which. 133. **Tread not upon him**: Difficult. Perhaps indicating that the mob is stomping on Martius's
corpse, or the line may be addressed to the guards, as in "Do not arrest Aufidius." 138. **cut off**: Put to
death. 141. **censure**: punishment. 144. **urn**: resting place. Martius will be buried honorably and with
great ceremony. —**His**: Martius'.

AUFIDIUS   My rage is gone,
      And I am struck with sorrow. Take him up.
      Help three o' th' chiefest soldiers; I'll be one.
      Beat thou the drum that it speak mournfully.
      Trail your steel pikes. Though in this city he   150
      Hath widowed and unchilded many a one,
      Which to this hour bewail the injury,
      Yet he shall have a noble memory.
      Assist.

                            Exeunt, bearing the body of Martius.

                                    A dead march sounded.

---

149. **speak mournfully**: a funeral dirge. 150. **Trail your steel pikes**: symbolizing a fallen comrade of arms. 151. **unchilded**: killed many sons, whose fathers and mothers mourn still, as expressed at 5.6.121-122, above.

How to Read
Coriolanus As Performance

Some may feel some reluctance to see *Coriolanus* as anything more than a text. After all, if a local troupe performs *Coriolanus* and adds a scene, cuts a line, or suits up in modern costume, we might argue that these enhancements have nothing to do with Shakespeare's own writing. Yet modern criticism now accepts that Shakespeare wrote his plays with the theater in mind, *and not just his theater*. Rather, it is now clear that Shakespeare wrote with the foreknowledge that his plays might be performed at the Globe, at Court, or in a variety of theatrical spaces during the occasional summer tour. In short, Shakespeare wrote his plays not necessarily with us in mind, but did write his plays knowing that they had to be flexible enough to adapt to a wide variety of theatrical conditions. This built-in flexibility allows directors to stay true to Shakespeare and to our modern sensibilities. In this short essay, we will be looking at many of those points of performative flexibility.

As *Coriolanus* begins, a group of rioters enter demanding food from the state. How would Shakespeare have staged the scene? We really don't know what kind of costumes would have been used to signify working-class plebeians. One thing we do know is that Shakespeare's actors did not always dress in setting-appropriate costume. There is no reason to suppose that everyone was in a toga, despite the fact that we're dealing with a Roman play. This flexibility of costume has given directors free reign. A 2002 RSC production (dir. David Farr) set the play to Samurai-style costume and music; likewise, a 2007 RSC production (dir. Yukio Ninagawa) opened on "huge… civic sets surmounted by Shinto statues of warriors posing in triumph."[1] For a 2008 production at the Oregon Shakespeare Festival, dir. Laird Williamson had a "stone slab with a jagged, metal fault-line splitting the performance space as clearly as Rome is split by her own political divisions."[2]

The crowd is out for blood, but one man faces them all down. It is Menenius, who, we might imagine, is dressed in aristocratic garb. He calms them down with his tale of the belly, and the mob seems ready to discuss things—until Martius arrives and stirs them with a series of insults. We might easily imagine the mob on one side,

---

1   Paul Taylor, *The Independent*, April 30, 2007.

2   *North Bay Bohemian*, June 16, 2008.

Martius on the other, but in so doing we might forget Menenius. Where does he stand, and what does his placement mean? If he stands next to Martius, he is opposed to the people of Rome; if he stands with the mob, then Martius is a lone voice against a livid Roman citizenry. Perhaps he stands midway, trying to placate both parties, his hands held up, like a traffic cop trying to avert a bad accident. Again, performance might give us a fuller sense of the play's possibilities: For the 1984 BBC TV version (dir. Elijah Moshinsky), a manicured Martius (Alan Howard) entered on horseback to outface a grimy common folk. Christopher Walken's Martius (New York's Public Theatre, 1988; dir. Steven Berkoff) was "a modern urbanite."[3] In his military fatigues, Tom McCamus (Stratford, Ontario, 1997; dir. Richard Rose) was both military hero and a "menacing pathological killer—equal parts momma's boy and megalomaniac, with a touch of homo-eroticism tossed in for good measure."[4] At the Olde Globe San Diego (2009; dir. Darko Tresnjak), Martius (Steven Marzolf, substituting for Greg Derelian) enters in military fatigues, with a cocked rifle, ready to fire into the mob.

And what of Martius and his stand-off with the plebeians? If Martius is utterly unarmed, then we have a sense of his confidence. If Martius enters with sword in hand, we have an authoritarian bully, secure only because he is better armed than his foes. At 1.1.206, a messenger enters with news of a war with the Volscians. Martius suggests to the crowd that they join him in battle. Again, only in performance will we get the full effect of the line. Is his offer genuine, a call for unity, or yet another insult? Does the mob go with him or skulk off? What is clear is that suddenly Martius is no longer a man unto himself. He is, rather, the center of Roman activity. In 1.4, for example, we see Martius delivering a crowd-cheering war speech. Still, Martius is not one to fight alongside Roman soldiers, preferring to see war not as a clash of competing military powers but as a test of personal honor and integrity. The result is that even in his triumph at Corioli, Martius sees the people of Rome as superfluous: "Alone I fought in ... Corioles walls/And made what work I pleas'd" (1.8.8-9). On the issue of personal honor and integrity, we might further note that Aufidius' inability to defeat Martius by legitimate *mano-a-mano* battle explains his later subterfuge in Act 5. If Audifius is to overcome Martius, brawn alone will not be enough. Directors have used a variety of props or, in some instances, sheer brawn to convey Martius' battle-hardened physicality: For example, Jonathan Cake's Martius (The Globe, London, 2006; dir. Dominic Dromgoole) was "a crowd-pleasing action hero, inspiring gasps as he conquers the Volscian foe like some full-scale version of Tom Cruise in *Mission Impossible CDCXCIII BC*."[5]

Act 2 continues the play's exploration of personal worth versus public acclaim. At 2.1.143, Martius re-enters Rome. Although Martius is publically feted, it is his reunion with his mother and his wife that occupies us visually. The stage direction calls for Martius to kneel to his mother but has no call for any embrace with his wife.

---

3   William Over, "The Public Theatre *Coriolanus.*" *SQ* 41 (1990): 365-68.

4   Robert Reid, *Kitchener-Waterloo Record*, June 30, 1997.

5   Kate Bassett, *The Independent*, May 20, 2006.

Does this suggest Martius' indifference to his wife, or does it imply his inability to express more than perfunctory affection before the eyes of strangers? In 2.2, Martius is truly uncomfortable with the public acclaim heaped on him. This is exacerbated in 2.3, in which Martius must put on the gown of humility and beg the people's favor. On paper, this may read simply as Martius' inflexible contempt for the plebeians, but live performance should highlight quite starkly how unlike the plebeians he really is. The gown of humility should be ill-fitting and slightly ridiculous on the arrogant and overweening Martius. Visually, we should understand that, culturally and even physically, Martius is in no way ordinary.

Where performance really opens our eyes to Martius, however, is in his relationship with his mother, particularly in 3.2, in which Volumnia convinces him to be more moderate with the people and, if necessary, to swallow his honor in order to achieve his ends. In reaction, Colm Feore's Martius (Stratford, Ontario, 2006; dir. Antonio Cimolino) "whines and shouts… looks at the floor when in trouble[;] he pouts, he rolls his eyes, … stomps away in a temper and caves under his mother's disapproval"; his mother (played by Martha Henry) displayed a "neurotic will," and "all but seduces her son with whispered pleadings and protestations."[6]

For anyone who has sent a child off to fight abroad or, still more commonly, remembers the separation anxiety of walking alone to school for the first time, Act 4 is perhaps the easiest to stage because it is in many ways the most natural. Volumnia is usually depicted as, by turns, tearful and wrathful; Virgilia is nearly silent except for her ineffective "O heavens! O heavens!" and "O the gods!" As he leads mother and wife to the gates of Rome, Martius himself is calm. The actual farewell is unstaged but the sight of them walking together has its own gravity.

4.4 shows the reverse. Martius enters Antium alone but, by the end of the scene, is embraced by the general who once called him foe. Readers, however, might miss some of the drama in between, particularly at 4.5.48: Martius has already entered muffled in rags, a result, no doubt, of his having traveled from Rome to Antium on foot. His head is obscured, possibly with a cloak or veil of some sort. At line 49, he unmuffles, no doubt slowly and dramatically. As we await Aufidius' reaction, there is invariably a holding of breath. Will Aufidius pick up a knife and kill the unarmed Martius then and there? No, instead, and this should surprise Martius as much as it does the audience, Aufidius embraces him.

One aspect of the play in performance we have not yet discussed is the speed of presentation. 4.6 should begin languidly: Sicinius and Brutus lolling festively through Rome, the city contented and pleased with itself. Even Menenius grudgingly admits that all is well. But bad news enters at line 37, followed by confirmation at line 56, again at line 73, and yet again at line 79. The patricians and tribunes react to the crisis with confusion, soon echoed by the people's own fear and growing fury at the tribunes who once so easily egged them on. 4.7, on the other hand, should show the deliberate, methodical nature of the Volscians and the calm certainty of Martius' re-

---

6   Robyn Godfrey, *Weekender* [Perth, Ontario], June 30, 2006; *Hamilton Spectator*, May 31, 2006.

venge. These two competing speeds are on display in 5.2, in which Menenius rushes to the Volscian camp, but the guard leisurely and confidently refuses his request to see Martius, who then enters, quite on accident, but still refuses Menenius' pleas with a brusque "Away!" (5.2.74)

Act 5, scene 3 should offer a variety of heartfelt scenes, perhaps not easily glimpsed off the page. Firstly, we have Martius' near-tearful confession to Aufidius that he turned away Menenius at some personal cost:

> This last old man,
> Whom with a crack'd heart I have sent to Rome,
> Lov'd me above the measure of a father;... (5.3.8-10)

The confession is followed quickly by the entry at line 21 of the Lady Valeria, Martius' mother Volumnia, his wife Virgilia, and his son. It is here that Young Martius has his moment. Although he has only two lines in the scene (5.3.127-28), his muted actions speak volumes. At 5.3.75, for example, his grandmother orders him to kneel, but we may infer he refuses, given Martius' reaction — "That's my brave [i.e. defiant] boy!" At line 170, along with the Lady Valeria and his grandmother, Young Martius falls to his knees. Martius at last relents, and Rome is safe. For the 1984 BBC TV version (dir Elijah Moshinsky), a tearful Martius (Alan Howard) slumped defeatedly. His mother (Irene Worth), while upset, understood the necessity of his sacrifice and held herself up with solemnity and discipline.

Shakespeare has given us very little direction on how to stage Martius' death, and, consequently, the scene has been freely interpreted. In the 1984 BBC TV version (dir Elijah Moshinsky), Martius (Alan Howard) allowed Aufidius (Mike Gwilym) to turn his blade against him and, thereby, assisted in his own disembowelment. He took an also orgasmic joy at his life's release. In Berkoff's 1988 production (New York's Public Theatre, 1988), Martius (Christopher Walken) was impaled on Volscian blades and finished off by Aufidus' sword.[1] In Steven Berkoff's 1991 version, Martius thrilled to hear the catalogue of those he had killed. He was thereafter encircled and stabbed by the Volscian lords; Aufidius administering a seemingly welcomed *coup de grace*. For a 2002 RSC production (dir. David Farr), Martius (Greg Hicks) was "felled by a cheating bullet from behind. Twice he drags himself to his feet to continue the contest and twice more he's shot."[2] At the Olde Globe, San Diego, 2009 (dir. Darko Tresnjak), Martius (Steven Marzolf, substituting for Greg Derelian) had his legs cut out from under him by one of Aufidius' seconds. Martius' rival merely finishes him off with a single bullet to the head.

While it is true that there may be no right or wrong to staging a Shakespeare, there is, too, no "final" way to stage a Shakespeare. Future productions of *Coriolanus* will only add to its rich legacy. Further points of performative interest, by some of the finest Shakespeare companies in the world, are highlighted in the Introduction and in the notes of this edition.

1   Lee Blissed, *Coriolanus* (Cambridge: Cambridge University Press, 2000. 95.

2   Paul Taylor, *The Independent*, December 4, 2002.

TIMELINE

Editor's note: Shakespeare almost certainly read of Caius Martius Coriolanus in Plutarch's *Parallel Lives*, which was translated into English by Thomas North in 1579. Despite Plutarch's high reputation as an historian, no dates are provided for this Roman, who may or may not have lived in the late 6th and early 5th centuries BC. Given the paucity of specific historical dates, this timeline addresses the violent nature of Shakespeare's world and why a figure like Coriolanus may have intrigued Shakespeare and his contemporaries. [J.K.]

1554   Jane Grey, *de facto* Queen of England for a brief period in 1553, and her husband Guildford Dudley were executed at the Tower of London. In the same year, the Protestants rebelled, led by Sir Thomas Wyatt the Younger. Wyatt was executed. Princess Elizabeth, the future Queen of England, was imprisoned in the Tower for eight weeks.

1555   Protestants in England are persecuted; 300 are burned at the stake.

1558   England loses Calais to the French; Queen Mary I dies; Queen Elizabeth crowned.

1560   The Siege of Leith: English troops besiege the French garrisoned in Scotland.

1563   Bubonic Plague in London: Queen Elizabeth I moves her court to Windsor Castle, orders that anyone coming from London be hanged.

1564   Shakespeare born.

1567   Mary, Queen of Scots is implicated in the death of her first husband and abdicates. Her son, James, is crowned King James VI.

1568   Mary, Queen of Scots, imprisoned in England.

1569   The Nevilles of Durham and Percys of Northumberland are executed for plotting rebellion.

1572   French Protestants are massacred by French Catholics in Paris on St. Bartholomew's Day.

1580   The Irish rebel against English rule: 46 leaders, 800 followers and 4,000 common folk are executed; 600 Spanish soldiers attempt to land in Ireland; they are captured and executed.

1581   Sir Francis Drake, Vice Admiral of the English fleet, attacks Spanish ships; King Philip II puts a bounty of 20,000 ducats on Drake (US$6.5M).

1582   The English refuse to let the Irish harvest their own fields, leading to the death by starvation of thousands. Shakespeare marries Anne Hathaway.

1583   Anne Hathaway gives birth to Shakespeare's daughter, Susanna.

1585   Queen Elizabeth takes the Netherlands under her protection; Spanish troops stationed there come under attack. Shakespeare's wife, Anne Hathaway, gives birth to twins, son Hamnet and daughter Judith.

1586   A plot to assassinate Queen Elizabeth and replace her with Mary, Queen of Scots, discovered. The leader of the plot, Anthony Babbington, is executed.

1587   Mary, Queen of Scots, executed; Spain declares war on England.

1588   The Spanish Armada, a large military fleet, is defeated by the English.

1588-1591 Shakespeare leaves for London, begins career as actor and playwright for a variety of companies. His initial success is with "The First Tetralogy," a series of plays (*1-3Henry VI* and *Richard III*) chronicling the bloody history of the English Civil War (1455 and 1485).

1593   Shakespeare writes *Titus Andronicus*, his first Roman play, a bloodbath of war, rape, mutilation, murder and cannibalism.

1595   English battles: Earl of Essex and Lord Howard of Effingham capture Cadiz, Spain; Sir Francis Drake launches an unsuccessful attack on San Juan, Puerto Rico, a Spanish settlement.

1596   Sir Francis Drake dies of dysentery. William Spenser defends the slaughter of the Irish in his book, *A View of the Present State of Ireland*. (It is registered for publication two years later, but is not published until 1633.)

1597   The Irish rebel; the English suppress the rebellion; Spain launches a second Armada against England; the ships are scattered in a storm.

1599   Earl of Essex is sent by Queen Elizabeth I to put down the Irish. He signs a truce and, upon his return to England, is arrested and imprisoned for his (non)action.

1599   Shakespeare writes *Julius Caesar*, a Roman play dealing with the assassination of Caesar (44BC) and the civil war that followed.

1595-1599 Shakespeare writes "The Second Tetralogy," a series of bloody plays chronicling the reigns of Richard II, Henry IV, Henry V (1377-1422).

1601   Essex attempts rebellion against Queen Elizabeth I. He is arrested, tried, and executed.

1603   Queen Elizabeth I dies; James VI of Scotland proclaimed James I of England.

1605   The Gunpowder Plot: Guy Fawkes and other Catholic conspirators attempt to blow up Parliament and James I.

1608:   Shakespeare writes *Coriolanus*.

1616   Shakespeare dies.

1618   Beginning of religious Thirty Years War in Central Europe.

1623   First Folio of Shakespeare's plays published, *Coriolanus* included.

Topics for Discussion and Further Study

Critical Issues

1. Martius goes through life with a sense of entitlement. Drawing on examples from the play, judge whether this is a weakness or a strength.

2. In tragedies, characters generally change in the course of a play. Compare the Martius of Act 1 with the Martius of Act 5. In what way has he changed? If he hasn't, what, in your view, can we say about his "nature"?

3. War in this play seems to be more about honor than territory, money, and power. Is war ever justified?

4. Compare the Roman scenes with the Volscian scenes. To what extent do the two enemies resemble each other? If they are not opposites, why are they fighting?

5. Women exert a powerful influence in the play. Do some research on the power women in ancient Rome actually had in the home and in Roman society.

6. Martius single-handedly storms Corioli. Are his acts brave or foolhardy?

7. Aufidius both hates and admires Martius. Is this a matter of jealousy? Study Aufidius' erotic language in 4.5.

8. Menenius stalls rebellion in 1.1 with his tale of the belly. Is his argument/story convincing? If not, why not?

9. In your view, are the plebeians justified in banishing Martius?

10. Martius questions the whether Roman society can function when its leaders say what they really think. What does this say about democracy, as Shakespeare understood it?

Performance Issues

1. Martius' father is nowhere to be found. Write a scenario in which he is killed in battle, or that he, still living, is the town drunk.

2. Do some research into the play's performance history. Find two versions of the play that seem to be at loggerheads with each other and present them to the class.

3. For all the war in the play, we see, surprisingly, little actual fighting. Note that even Martius' greatest victory at Corioli is to a great extent reported. What reason might Shakespeare have for *not* staging battle scenes?

4. If we were to stage the play with women playing all the roles, how would we view the play differently?

5. Watch the BBC *Coriolanus*. The director has purposely cut many lines and transitions out of the play. Now do the opposite. Write a new scene and insert it into the script. How are you affecting pace and characterization? Is it possible to imitate or even improve Shakespeare?

6. Restage the play in World War II, with Martius as a fighter pilot. What difference does it make if Martius does not face the enemy in hand-to-hand combat?

7. Stage Martius' conquest of Corioli but use some farcical or vaudevillian music as a soundtrack. How can the addition of music work as counterpoint to the text?

8. Imagine you were casting a film of *Coriolanus*. What famous actors or celebrities would you choose for each role and why?

9. *Coriolanus* is, essentially, a gladiator movie. Compare and contrast it with one other recent movie of this genre — i.e. Russell Crowe in Ridley Scott's *Gladiator* (2000).

10. The peasant class claims that Martius does all to please his mother. Yet, to please his mother, Martius must die. Revise the play so that Volumnia is the true and clear villain.

BIBLIOGRAPHY

The following is a selective and by no means exhaustive list of criticism to aid the student. The following texts are widely available online or in college or university libraries.

Berry, Ralph "Sexual Imagery in *Coriolanus*." *Studies in English Literature*, 1500-1900 13.2 (Spring, 1973), pp. 301-316.

> Berry argues that both "Aufidius and [Martius] react to victory with a metaphor of heterosexual triumph," and that Shakespeare suggests, though he does not state, "the possibility of a homosexual attachment" between the heroes.

Honigmann, E.A.J. *Shakespeare: The Dramatist's Manipulation of Response*. Houndsmills, Basingstoke, Hampshire and New York: Palgrave/Macmillan, 1976; rpt. 2002. pp. 170-191.

> Honigmann argues that Martius, in sacrificing himself, grows beyond his proud and stubborn personality, but, in confronting Aufidius at the play's close, reverts to his old self — an end which Honigmann finds "all the more pitiful."

Hazlitt, William *Hazlitt on Theatre*. New York: Hill and Wang, [1957].

> In his discussion of *Coriolanus*, Hazlitt writes that "the language of poetry naturally falls in with the language of power. ... The principle of poetry is a very anti-leveling principle." As such, he feels that the play seduces the reader or audience against the just claims of a starving people: "We had rather be the oppressor than the oppressed."

Johnson, Samuel *Johnson on Shakespeare*. Ed. Walter Raleigh. Oxford: Oxford University Press, 1908; rpt. 1959. p.178.

> Johnson suggests that Rome's plebeians fully reflect Shakespeare's personal thoughts on democracy and mob mentality.

Oliver, H. J. "Coriolanus As Tragic Hero." *Shakespeare Quarterly* 10.1 (Winter, 1959), pp. 53-60.

Oliver believes the play has been neglected critically because of "a failure to interpret sympathetically the character of the hero." In Oliver's view, Shakespeare has gone out of his way to humanize Martius, who, by the play's close, must choose between mercy for Rome and honor for himself. To his credit, he chooses mercy.

Olsen, Thomas G. "Apolitical Shakespeare; Or, the Restoration *Coriolanus*." *Studies in English Literature*, 1500-1900 38.3 (Summer, 1998), pp. 411-425.

Olsen argues that Tate's The *Ingratitude of a Common-Wealth; Or, The Fall of Caius Martius Coriolanus* (1681) represents a critical moment in the "development of several important Restoration aesthetic and political tendencies"; specifically, it "promotes an antidemocratic orthodoxy that Shakespeare's original avoids."

Rabkin, Norman "The Tragedy of Politics." *Shakespeare Quarterly* 17.3 (Summer, 1966), pp. 195-212.

Despite the title, the article concerns Martius, who is, in Rabkin's view, motivated by "a neurosis." The reader or viewer must wrestle with the (possible) relationship of moral principle to personal pathology.

Ripley, John "*Coriolanus*'s Stage Imagery on Stage, 1754-1901." *Shakespeare Quarterly* 38.3 (Autumn, 1987), pp. 338-350.

Ripley is interested in the visual motifs of the play, as staged in the eighteenth and nineteenth centuries.

Sheldon, Esther K. Sheridan's *Coriolanus*: An 18th-Century Compromise." *Shakespeare Quarterly* 14.2 (Spring, 1963), pp. 153-161.

This article offers a reading of Thomas Sheridan's adaptation, performed in Dublin in 1752. The key point is that in this version Martius loved the people but hated their cowardly and conniving representatives.

Stockholder, Katherine "The Other Coriolanus." *PMLA* 85.2 (Mar., 1970), pp. 228-236.

Stockholder places the blame for Martius' shortcomings on his mother, who has created a mamma's boy who prides himself on his independence.

Tolman, Albert H. "Is Shakespeare Aristocratic?" *PMLA* 29.3(1914), pp. 277-298.

Citing passages from *Coriolanus*, Tolman argues that Shakespeare "favored the monarchy and the nobility," and was, consequently, "opposed to increasing the power of the people."

Tupper, Jr. , Frederick The Shakesperean Mob." *PMLA* 27.4 (1912), pp. 486-523.

Tupper agrees that Shakespeare's mobs are fickle, dangerous and stupid, but does that mean that we have here a reflection of Shakespeare's personal political views? No, argues Tupper, who suggests that Shakespeare was merely following then-current conventions of stage and of print.

Waith, Eugene M. "Manhood and Valor in Two Shakespearean Tragedies." *ELH* 17.4 (Dec., 1950), pp. 262-273.

This article looks at a variety of Roman, medieval and Renaissance texts to argue that "true manhood is a comprehensive ideal, growing out of the familiar Christian concept that man is between the beast and the angels in the hierarchy of creation."

FILMOGRAPHY

Coriolanus (1951). Dir. Paul Nickell; Martius: Richard Greene; Volumnia: Judith Evelyn. Black and white video. Approx. 60 minutes.

> Jack Gould of the *New York Times* called it "not very exciting"; Richard Greene's Martius was "virtually expressionless." The production as a whole lacks dramatic unity.

Coriolanus (1984). Dir. Elijah Moshinsky; Martius: Alan Howard; Volumnia: Irene Worth. Color. Available on DVD. 145 minutes.

> The BBC's 1984 TV version is ambitious but, ultimately, fails due to a lack of coherence and poor production values. The play is set in seventeenth-century Holland and looks, in many scenes, to be straight out of any number of Johan Vermeer paintings, but this begs the question why the Dutch would act like Romans or vice versa. The video is marred throughout with quick cuts, which produces a feeling of discenteredness. We are just getting comfortable in one scene, when, snip! — we find ourselves in another.

Coriolanus (1997). Dir. Steven Berkoff; Martius: Steven Berkoff; Volumnia: Linda Marlowe. Filmed at the Tokyo Globe Theatre. Color. Approx 144 minutes. DVD release: 2004.

> This is, essentially, a filmed version of a stage production, with a few added tight shots. The production features Berkoff's signature slow-motion fight scenes and a minimum of scenery. Once the viewer accepts that the acting is not naturalistic, the performances are powerful throughout.

Coriolanus (2011). Dir. Ralph Fiennes; Martius: Ralph Fiennes; Aufidius: Gerard Butler; Volumnia: Vanessa Redgrave. Hermetof Pictures, Magna Films, Icon Entertainment International Approx 122 minutes.

> Despite the popularity of traditional and pseudo-Roman settings on television (*Spartacus*), film (*Gladiator*), and in literature (*Game of Thrones*), no major TV or film production of *Coriolanus* has yet opted for the traditional setting of ancient Rome. In this 2011 film, we have a fairly modern spin on the play, set in what looks to be the Balkans.

Rome is here a place of grim disarray and ripe for urban warfare. We
see a group of multinationals (the working poor?) meeting with a
community organizer. A peaceful rally ensues, but when talk of murder
comes up, hardly an eyebrow is raised. This is to be expected, given the
government's black-booted, baton-wielding response to cries for more
bread. In Shakespeare's version, Menenius calms the restless crowd,
but here the elder statesman is a slightly malevolent TV personality
(Brian Cox), who prefers expensive restaurants to mingling among
the masses. Ralph Fiennes's Martius, while hardly an imposing figure,
is contemptuous, straightforward, and itching for a fight: "He who
deserves greatness deserves your hate." Dressed in a gown of humility
(here re-tailored from toga to cheap suit), he is by turns sarcastic and
frank, but the city dwellers of this Rome are far from humble and
have had their fill of humiliation. Their options, however, are limited.
The rival Volscian city, Antium, is a place of underground bunkers,
torture, and execution. Their leader Aufidius (Gerard Butler) is, if
anything, more bloodthirsty than his Roman counterpart. The muted
colors of the film suggest the brutal and basic, but this limited palette
sometimes clashes against Shakespeare's complex language and poetry.